Johanna Schwarz

Patchwork Knitting

18 Projects to Knit and Crochet

Schiffer Publishing Ltd
4880 Lower Valley Road • Atglen, PA 19310

Schiffer Books are available at special discounts for bulk purchases for sales promotions or premiums. Special editions, including personalized covers, corporate imprints, and excerpts can be created in large quantities for special needs. For more information contact the publisher:

Published by Schiffer Publishing Ltd.
4880 Lower Valley Road
Atglen, PA 19310
Phone: (610) 593-1777; Fax: (610) 593-2002
E-mail: Info@schifferbooks.com

For the largest selection of fine reference books on this and related subjects, please visit our website at
www.schifferbooks.com
We are always looking for people to write books on new and related subjects. If you have an idea for a book, please contact us at
proposals@schifferbooks.com

This book may be purchased from the publisher.
Please try your bookstore first.
You may write for a free catalog.

In Europe, Schiffer books are distributed by
Bushwood Books
6 Marksbury Ave.
Kew Gardens
Surrey TW9 4JF England
Phone: 44 (0) 20 8392 8585; Fax: 44 (0) 20 8392 9876
E-mail: info@bushwoodbooks.co.uk
Website: www.bushwoodbooks.co.uk

Originally published 2010
by Christophorus Verlag GmbH & Co. KG Freiburg
Translated by Carol Rhoades
Technical advisor for the English edition: Anita Closic

Library of Congress Control Number: 2012932850

Concept, Design, and Realization: Johanna Schwarz
Photographs: Uwe Schotte
Styling: Ilka Baumgarten
Technical Illustrations: Jana Schwarz
Crochet diagrams: Sabine Schidelko

ISBN: 978-0-7643-4092-5
Printed in China

Dear Readers!

Originally a Chemist, Johanna Schwarz worked in the research and development of textile manufacturing until 1988. Her passion for handicraft prompted her to complete textile designer training at the Cultural Academy in Halle. She has been independent since 1989 and opened her own knitting and design school in Halle.

Before I could read and write, I had already knitted my first stitch. Since then I have loved handicraft, and, with time, I developed new ideas to construct models more creatively. For this, I often used wool remnants because throwing away beautiful yarn was out of the question for me. I always sorted my treasures according to color and thickness, newly combined them, and created distinctive, individual pieces. Thus, the "knitting kit" was formed.

Here, it is not only a matter of using leftovers. With the knitting kit, the fun of creating is at the forefront: fantastic yarn, stylish colors, and geometric shapes merge together to make a complete work of art. Thus, there is no limit to creativity because each model can be individually varied.

The path to a dream model is surprisingly simple: Knit single rectangles and squares that you join with a decorative crochet seam. Thanks to the diagrams and precise instructions, even novices can achieve stitching success step by step. In the chapter "Basics and General Tips," you will read everything you need to know about the technique; then you can begin immediately.

I wish you much fun in creating your favorite models!

Yours,

Contents

Basics and General Tips

What is Patchwork Knitting?

Individual pieces shaped as squares, rectangles, triangles, or trapezoids are knitted (also called "patches"), where "holes" from yarn overs and knitted together stitches are worked all around, close to the edge. These individual pieces are crocheted together according to a diagram for each displayed model. The holes serve as the basis for the decorative crochet seam; the single crochet stitches are worked into them so that the crochet seam runs evenly between all individual pieces and always has the same distance to the border. A correct fit is guaranteed, and it is also easy to combine differently sized individual pieces with each other.

Material

The material for the models displayed is specified in the instructions. However, you can also use your own yarn or wool remnants for knitting individual pieces. To ensure that the same fit is obtained with other yarn, you should knit a stitch gauge and compare this with the stitch gauge of the model. For this, knit a test sample with approximately 6 more stitches and rows than specified in the stitch gauge of the model. Using a measuring tape, count the stitches and rows to 4" (10 cm). If your stitch gauge has fewer stitches and rows than specified, you should work with thinner needles. If there are more stitches and rows, switch to thicker needles.

Note: The individual pieces cannot always be estimated according to the stitch gauge, because when you crochet them together, they are stretched in width or height. It is important that two individual pieces that are joined with each other show the same number of holes on the respective edges.

Knitting the Individual Pieces

For each model there is a clear table that correspondingly lists the individual pieces to be knitted with the number of their holes. Here, it is also specified how many of an individual piece will be required, how many stitches will be cast on, and how many rows will be knitted. Thus, you can immediately begin working.

Basic Pattern

Always knit the stockinette stitch: Knit stitches in the right side row, purl stitches in the wrong side row, each without edge stitches. The stockinette stitches appear on the wrongside as reverse stockinette stitches. Normally, the individual pieces are crocheted together in such a way that the stockinette on the model is right side of the work. However, for some models, individual pieces with the reverse stockinette are worked right side to achieve a mixture of designs and textiles. This is specified in the instructions.

All individual pieces that are to be knitted are marked according to the number of their holes:

General knitting chart for squares and rectangles

Example: Individual piece 7 x 7 (7 holes x 7 holes)

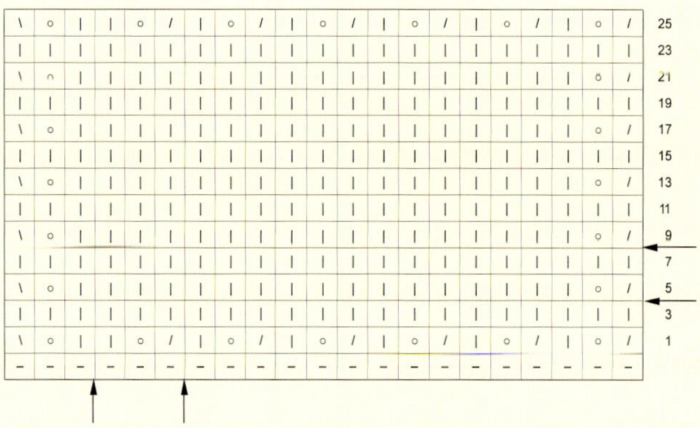

1 pattern repeat = 4 rows = 1 hole (Always repeated until the desired number of holes is reached)

1 pattern repeat = 3 stitches = 1 hole (Always repeated until the desired number of holes is reached)

All squares and rectangles are worked according to this general knitting chart example that shows the 1st wrong side row after the cast on and all following right side rows. Purl all stitches and yarn overs in the wrong side rows. After the last wrong side row cast off all knit stitches.

Tip: If the holes should be somewhat less noticeable, purl in the back of the loop in the wrong side row! Let the beginning and ending yarn of the individual pieces hang and include them into the crochet edge later when crocheting over the edges according to the tip on page 9.

For triangles, trapezoids, or other irregular shapes that are needed for necklines, collars, sleeves, and gusset pieces, separate knitting charts are always given in the description of the respective model. Their designation is as seen below:

Always use the stockinette stitch for the irregular individual pieces. Like with the general knitting chart for squares and rectangles, the pattern repeat always includes 3 stitches. It will be specified in the instructions how often it should be knitted. The rows are always completely illustrated.

Example: Irregular individual piece 3 x 3 x 2

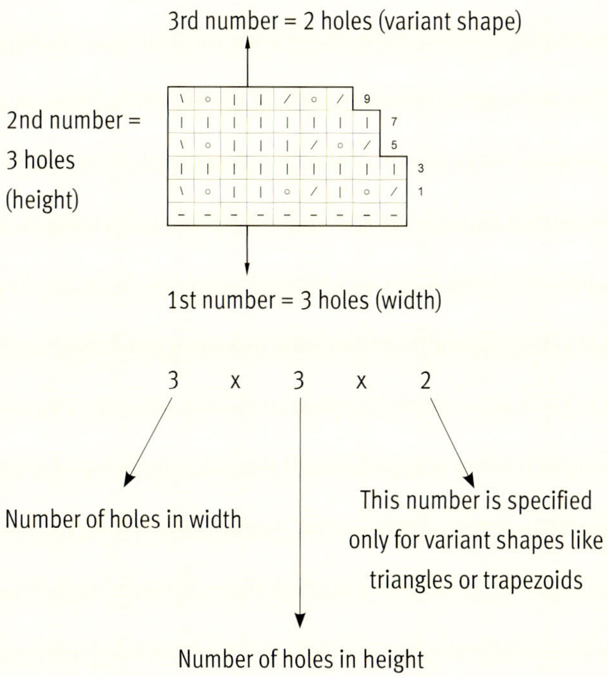

Key for Knitting Charts

[-] = Purl backward row after the cast on (not counted)

[I] = Knit stitch

[/] = Knit 2 together (k2tog)

[\] = Slip stitch knitwise, knit 1 stitch, pass the slipped stitch over the knitted stitch

[○] = 1 yarn over

Joining the Individual Pieces

When all pieces are knitted, they are joined with a decorative "seam." This can happen by crocheting together, or also by sewing together, for example, with satin ribbon, ribbon yarn, or leather strips. The preferred method in this book is crocheting. The selection of crochet yarn and the lines of the crochet junctions represent an additional element of the design. For example, crochet junctions that pick up the colors of the knitted individual pieces have a different optical effect than crochet junctions made of contrasting colored yarn. This allows for a unique, one-of-a-kind garment. For a better overview, it is recommended to first arrange all individual pieces according to the corresponding diagram and then begin joining the pieces.

Joining According to the Diagram

Joining the individual pieces takes place according to the respective diagram. The general crochet diagram on page 8 illustrates the process. Crocheting is done, as usual, from right to left. After joining an edge between two individual pieces, you will need to turn the piece in order to crochet in the correct direction. In addition to the respective diagram, the written instructions for "Joining the Individual Pieces," give detailed crochet instructions. Points with letters serve as the orientation. The crochet path described should make it possible to join the individual pieces consecutively without cutting off the working yarn. This eliminates the hassle of weaving in the yarn later. However, if the yarn has to be cut off at the end of a section, this is mentioned. If the described method seems somewhat confusing at first glance, it will quickly become clear during crocheting how the model comes together step by step. Normally, the junction points are no longer mentioned; they will be worked after the course on page 9.

1st step: **Preparation**

First crochet three sides of piece 1.

This step is called **preparation.**

During **preparation** in each hole crochet 1 single crochet stitch, 1 chain stitch, 1 single crochet stitch, and 1 chain stitch; these 4 stitches per hole are referred to as a cluster. In the corner holes crochet 2 clusters (= 1 cluster each per side). Turn the work with the last chain stitch at the end of an edge. Following the working direction, piece 2 will be added. Always position the piece that is to be added with the same side facing as on the preceding piece, thus, placing pieces with the wrong sides or right sides side by side.

2nd step: **Preparation and closing**

In the 2nd step, the edge of piece 2 that is not yet crocheted is prepared and joined with piece 1 at the same time.This step is therefore called **"preparation and closing."** First, crochet the 1st hole of piece 2 with 1 cluster, then work 1 single crochet stitch in the adjoining crochet edge of piece 1, in the process work this single crochet stitch around the last chain stitch of a cluster – this joining stitch is referred to as a **"connecting single crochet stitch,"** then crochet the following hole with 1 cluster, and repeat until the edges are joined, end with 1 connecting single crochet stitch around the corner chain stitch of piece 1. Next, prepare the second edge of piece 2. In the same way, crochet on pieces 3 to 5, working the junctions as is described on page 9.

General crochet diagram

Beginning

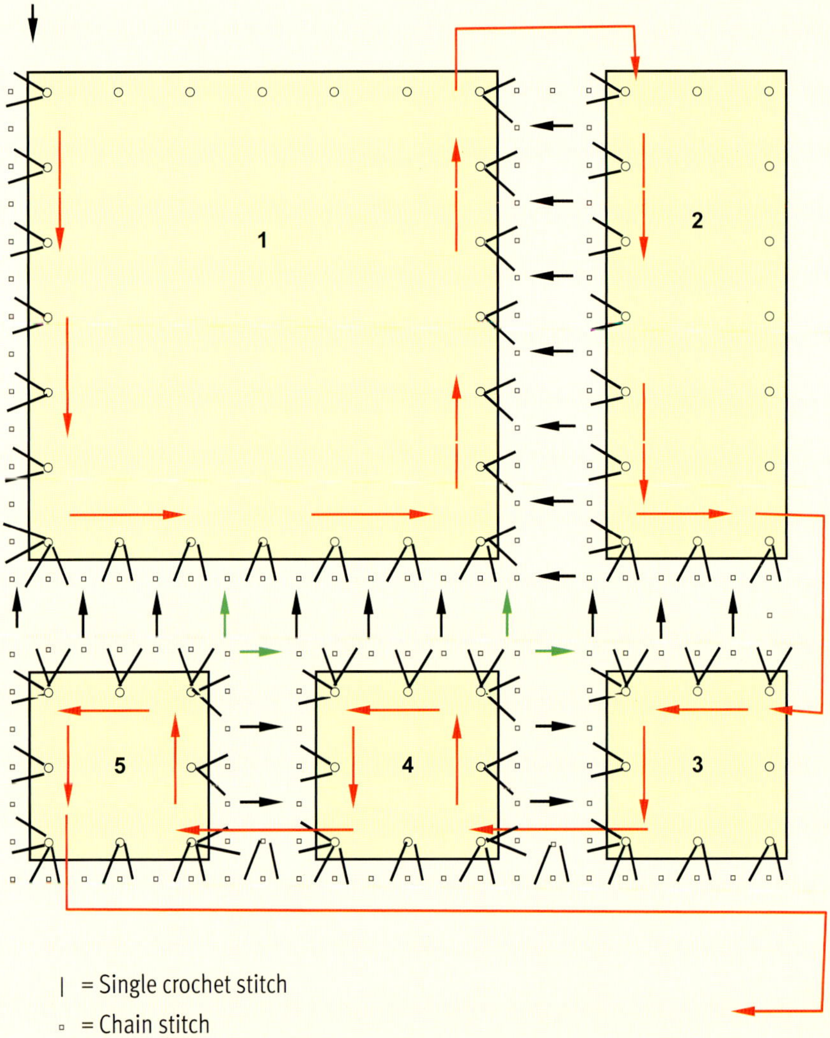

| = Single crochet stitch

▫ = Chain stitch

↑ = "Connecting single crochet stitch" (worked around the chain stitch of the connecting piece that is already crocheted around)

↑ = "Connecting single crochet stitch" for junctions

→ = Working direction (1→ 2→ 3 → 4→ 5...)

Preparation and Closing

One side must always be crocheted (prepared), before an additional piece that is not yet crocheted can be attached by preparation and closing. Then, after each preparation and closing, the next edge must again be prepared before another piece can be joined.

Junction

When four pieces meet (pieces 1, 2, 3, and 4 on the general crochet diagram), a junction develops. For this, after joining pieces 3 and 4, work a connecting single crochet stitch in the corner of piece 3 and a connecting single crochet stitch in the corner of piece 1 (see green arrows).

T-Junction

When 2 pieces meet a continuous edge (pieces 1, 4, and 5), a connecting single crochet stitch is crocheted around the corner chain stitch of piece 4 and a connecting single crochet stitch around the adjoining chain stitch of piece 1. The completed crocheted junction between pieces 5 and 4 is counted as a hole.

Edge Finish

When all five pieces are crocheted together, the holes of pieces 5, 4, and 3 are prepared with a cluster each, making sure that the crocheted junction between two individual pieces is always handled as a hole. This means that it is likewise crocheted with a cluster. The preparation serves as an edge finish when a model is completed.

Finished Block

The first block made from pieces 1 through 5 (see general crochet diagram) is finished.

Tip: To avoid the hassle of weaving in the ends of yarn of the individual pieces, these are included in the crochet edge as follows: First, place the yarn behind the work, and when crocheting the following single crochet stitch, including it in its "feet." Bring the yarn back forward, place the yarn back between the needle and working yarn, and work the chain stitch, thus the yarn will be kept invisible under the chain stitch. Continue repeating both steps until the yarn is tightly in the crochet stitches, finishing with a single crochet stitch. Then cut off the remaining short bit of yarn.

Course in Slippers

Joining the Sole and Toe (Diagram 1)

Prepare piece 1 on three edges (photograph 1), working 2 clusters = 1 cluster per edge in the corner holes. Turn the piece.

A small, but fine, model in the knitting kit system: I present the slippers to you. Their exceptionality is in the manner in which they are crocheted together. This is explained in the following course pages step by step and with clear photographs. You will find the yarn and knitting instructions, as well as the table of individual pieces on pages 58-59, and an additional, slightly modified model on pages 56-57.

Diagram 1

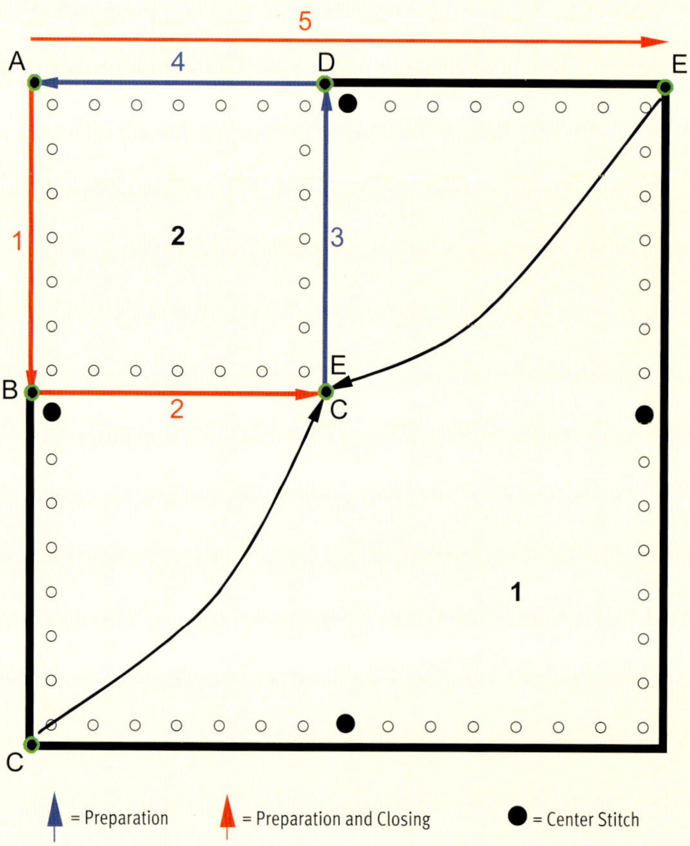

Step 1 (Red arrow 1)

Place piece 2 onto piece 1 with the wrong sides together. Join piece 2 and piece 1 on an edge from A to B by preparation and closing (photograph 2).

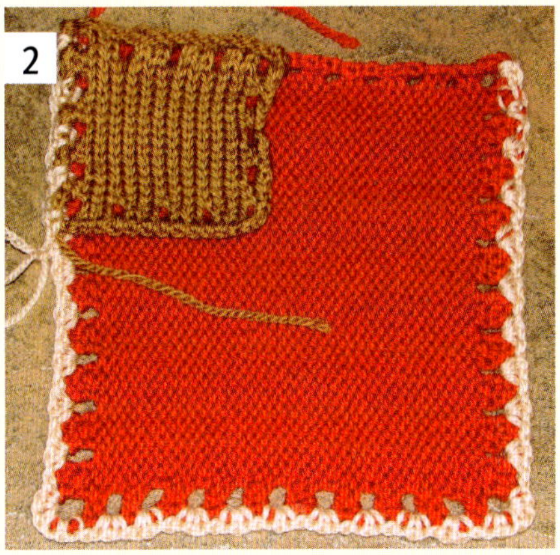

At B, piece 1, work a turn. For this, crochet a connecting single crochet stitch around the chain stitch after the cluster of the first center hole of piece 1 (photograph 3).

Then crochet 1 an additional connecting single crochet stitch into the previous cluster of piece 1 (photograph 4). This step is necessary because the crocheted connecting row must be handled as 1 hole. This is the only way it can be turned to switch to the next edge (photograph 5).

Step 2 (Red arrow 2)

Fold in corner C of piece 1; the points C of piece 1 and 2 meet. Join the second edge of piece 2 with the folded edge of piece 1 from B to C by preparation and closing (photograph 6).

Steps 3 and 4 (Blue arrows 3 and 4)

Prepare the third and fourth edge of piece 2 (photograph 7). Work a slip stitch through the beginning stitch so that there is no interruption.

Step 5 (Red arrow 5)

Join piece 1 and piece 2 from A to D. For the turn, crochet the center hole of piece 1 with a cluster. Then work 1 connecting single crochet stitch in the corner stitch of piece 2. Fold in the corner E of piece 1; the points E from piece 1 and piece 2 meet. Join piece 2 and piece 1 from D to E. Finish with 1 slip stitch in the 1st single crochet stitch of piece 1 (photograph 8).

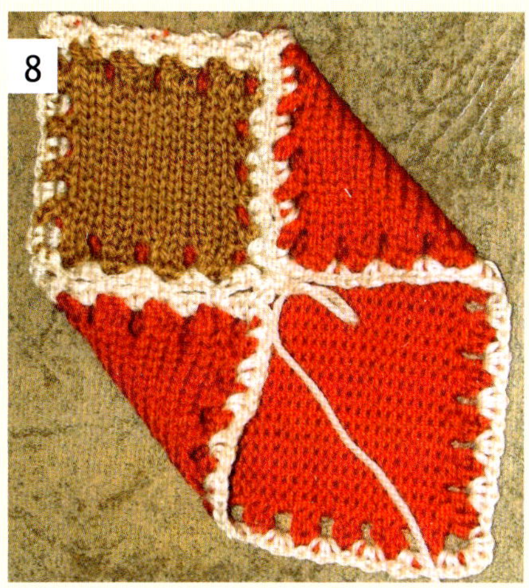

Joining the 1st Side Piece and Heel (Diagram 2)

Work the side piece 4 with an edge on the sole piece 1 and with the second edge on the heel piece 3.

Steps 6 (Red arrow 6) and 7 (Blue arrow 7)

Place piece 4 onto piece 1 with the right sides together, and join on an edge from A to B. Then prepare the second edge of piece 4 from D to C (photograph 9). Turn the shoe; reverse stockinette is outside.

9

Step 8 (Red arrow 8)

Join the heel piece 3 with the reverse stockinette outside on an edge with side piece 4 from C to D. Finish with a T-Junction. For this, work the last connecting single crochet stitch around the corner chain stitch of piece 4, and directly work another connecting single crochet stitch around the next chain stitch of piece 1 (photograph 10). This junction is counted as 1 hole.

10

Steps 9 and 10 (Red arrows 9 and 10)

Join the second edge of piece 3 from D up to the corner stitch with piece 1 and join the third edge of piece 3 from the corner stitch up to F with the following half edge of piece 1 (photograph 11).

Note: For the photographs 11, 13, and 14, the slipper was turned for a better view. When joining, however, the reverse stockinette is outside.

11

Step 11 (Blue arrow 11)

Prepare the fourth edge of piece 3 from F to E.

Joining the 2nd Side Piece

The second side piece 5 is worked in between the heel piece 3 and sole piece 1.

Step 12 (Red arrow 12)

The working yarn is located at E, piece 3. Turn the slipper; the stockinette is outside. Place the side piece 5 onto piece 3 with the right sides together and join pieces 5 and 3 on an edge from E to F. Finish with 1 connecting single crochet stitch in the corner of piece 3.

Step 13 (Red arrow 13)

For the following T-Junction, work 1 connecting single crochet stitch around the following free chain stitch of piece 1 (photograph 12). Then join the following edge of piece 5 with the last free edge of piece 1 (photograph 13). The same points G and H on the diagram meet.

12

13

Finally, prepare the free edges of the pieces 5 and 4 from H over E/C to A; finish with 1 connecting single crochet stitch in the edge of piece 3 (photograph 14). Cut off the yarn.

14

Diagram 2

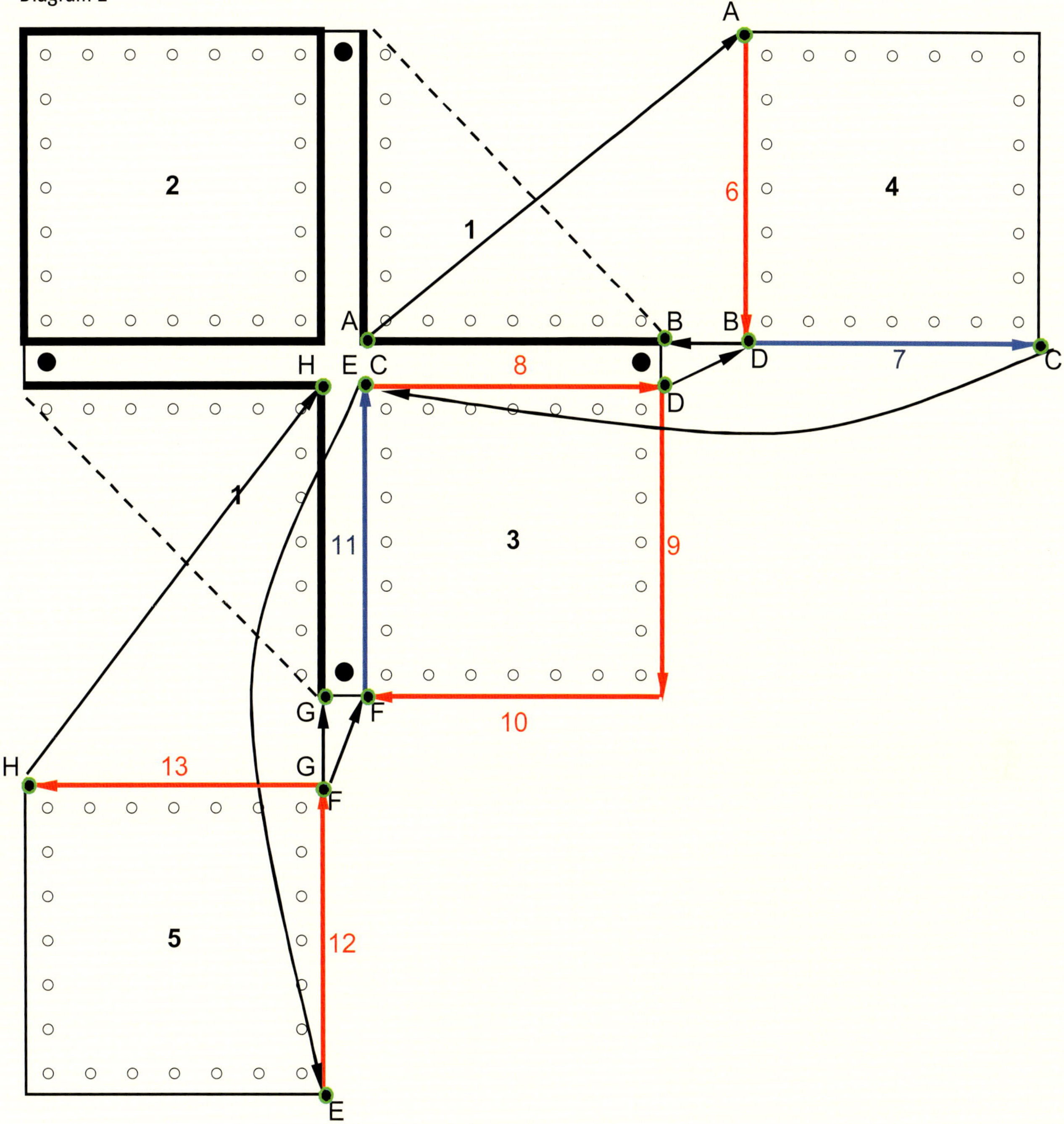

Wonderfully Comfortable

Flared Skirt in Trendy Black

Level of difficulty: Intermediate
Size: Sm: 36/38 {M: 40/42, Lg: 44/46}
Materials: Wick yarn (46% merino wool, 28% bamboo, 12% cotton, 7% baby alpaca, 7% super kid mohair), or substitute any chunky yarn that knits to gauge; $1^{3}/_{4}$ oz (50g)/100m (110 yds per skein). Black: Sm: 8 skeins [14 oz(400g), 880 yds] {M: 9 skeins [$15^{3}/_{4}$ oz (450g), 990 yds]; Lg: 10 skeins [17½ oz (500g), 1100 yds]}; purple, pink, green, and brown: 1 skein each [$1^{3}/_{4}$ oz (50g); 110yds, each]. Black elastic band in waist measurement, $^{3}/_{4}$" (2 cm) wide.
Knitting needles: US 10 (6mm)
Crochet hook: US J/10 (6mm)
Basic pattern: Stockinette stitch
Stitch gauge: 12 stitches and 20 rows = 4" x 4" (10 cm x 10 cm)

1. Knitting the Individual Pieces

According to the table, knit 12 different individual pieces at the specified quantity = 30 pieces. The number of stitches and rows, as well as the color and application of the pieces are specified. Knit according to the general knitting chart for squares and rectangles (see page 6), except for pieces 1 and 2. Work these pieces according to the knitting chart on page 16; in the process, work the pattern repeat for piece 1 for all sizes 3 times and for piece 2, work the pattern repeat 3 {5, 7} times.

2. Joining the Individual Pieces

Arrange the individual pieces according to the diagram; for the hem, place two of piece 3 or two of piece 4 on top of each other with the wrong sides together and work doubled. Arrows on the diagram = working direction of the individual pieces. Crochet together the individual pieces in black according to the general crochet diagrams on pages 8 and 16. The same points on the diagram meet. Two pieces are always joined by preparation and closing (see pages 8 - 9), even if this is not always explicitly mentioned in the text.

Joining the 1st Skirt Panel

Begin at A piece 9: Prepare three edges over B and C to D. Join piece 10 with piece 9 from D to C by preparation and closing; prepare an edge of piece 10 to E. Join the pieces 10 and 9 from E to B with piece 1; prepare two edges of piece 1 over F to G. Double two of piece 3 with the wrong sides together and join together with piece 1 from G to F. Then combine three edges of the doubled piece 3 to G by preparation. Prepare the edges of piece 1 and 10 to H.

Attaching the Other Skirt Panels

Join piece 7 with piece 10 from H to E, then prepare two edges of piece 7 to J. Join piece 8 with piece 7 from J to I. Prepare an edge of piece 8 to K. Join the pieces 8 and 7 from K to E with piece 2; work a junction to the pieces 7

		Holes			Cast on			Number of Rows			Stitches at the End to Cast Off				
Piece	Number	36/38	40/42	44/46	36/38	40/42	44/46	36/38	40/42	44/46	36/38	40/42	44/46	Color	Application
1	4	9 x 23 x 5	9 x 23 x 5	9 x 23 x 5	27	27	27	90	90	90	15	15	15	Black	Skirt panel / side *
2	2	9 x 23 x 5	11 x 23 x 7	13 x 23 x 9	27	33	39	90	90	90	15	21	27	Black	Skirt panel / center *
3	8	5 x 9	5 x 9	5 x 9	15	15	15	34	34	34	15	15	15	Black	Hem / center
4	4	5 x 9	5 x 11	5 x 13	15	15	15	34	42	50	15	15	15	Black	Hem / side
5	1	2 x 4	3 x 4	4 x 4	6	9	12	14	14	14	6	9	12	Purple	Waistband / center
6	1	2 x 4	3 x 4	4 x 4	6	9	12	14	14	14	6	9	12	Pink	Waistband / center
7	1	2 x 4	3 x 4	4 x 4	6	9	12	14	14	14	6	9	12	Green	Waistband / center
8	1	2 x 4	3 x 4	4 x 4	6	9	12	14	14	14	6	9	12	Brown	Waistband / center
9	2	2 x 4	2 x 4	2 x 4	6	6	6	14	14	14	6	6	6	Purple	Waistband / side
10	2	2 x 4	2 x 4	2 x 4	6	6	6	14	14	14	6	6	6	Pink	Waistband / side
11	2	2 x 4	2 x 4	2 x 4	6	6	6	14	14	14	6	6	6	Green	Waistband / side
12	2	2 x 4	2 x 4	2 x 4	6	6	6	14	14	14	6	6	6	Brown	Waistband / side

* Worked according to the knitting chart

and 1 (see page 9), and join piece 2 with piece 1; then prepare an edge of piece 2 to L. Double two of piece 4 with the wrong sides together and join together with piece 2 from L to G and with piece 3 from G to N. Combine the remaining two edges of the doubled piece 4 by preparation; then prepare the edges of piece 2 and 8 to M.

Likewise, attach the waistband, skirt panel, and hem pieces. After the last skirt panel from O, also join the pieces 3, 1, and 12 with the first pieces 3, 1, and 9 to A and thus join the skirt to form a circle. Cut off the yarn.

3. Finishing

Join a new skein of yarn at O and crochet the hem edge all around with a round of reverse single crochets (= single crochet stitches from left to right) in black. Hem the waistband inside, leaving an opening for the inclusion of the elastic band. Thread the elastic band in waist opening; sew the ends together and close the opening.

Knitting Chart

Piece 1 and 2

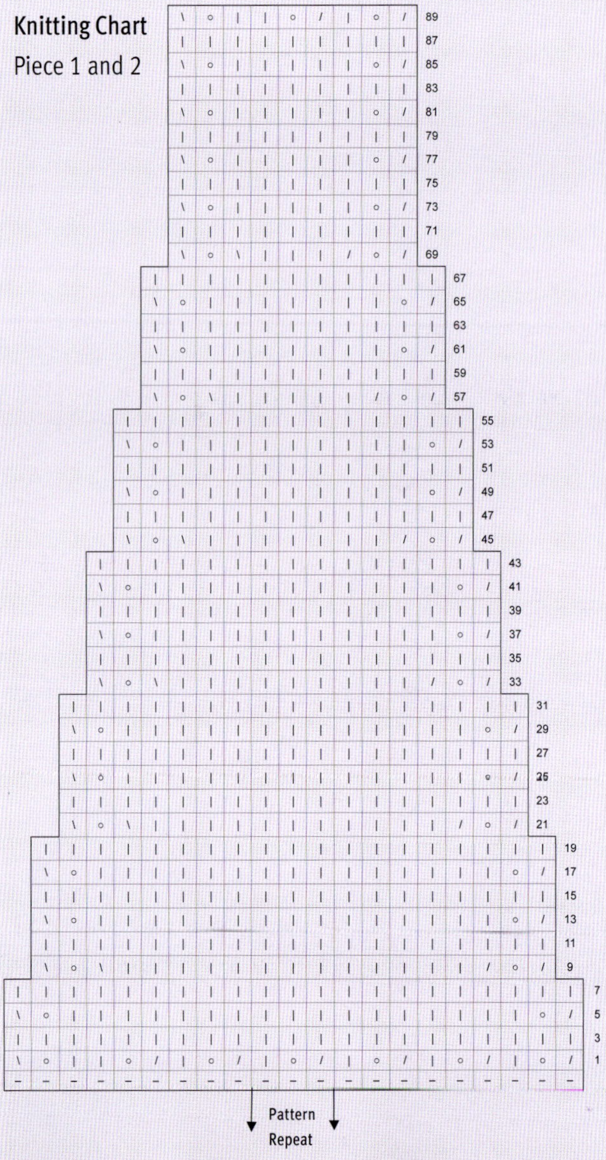

Diagram

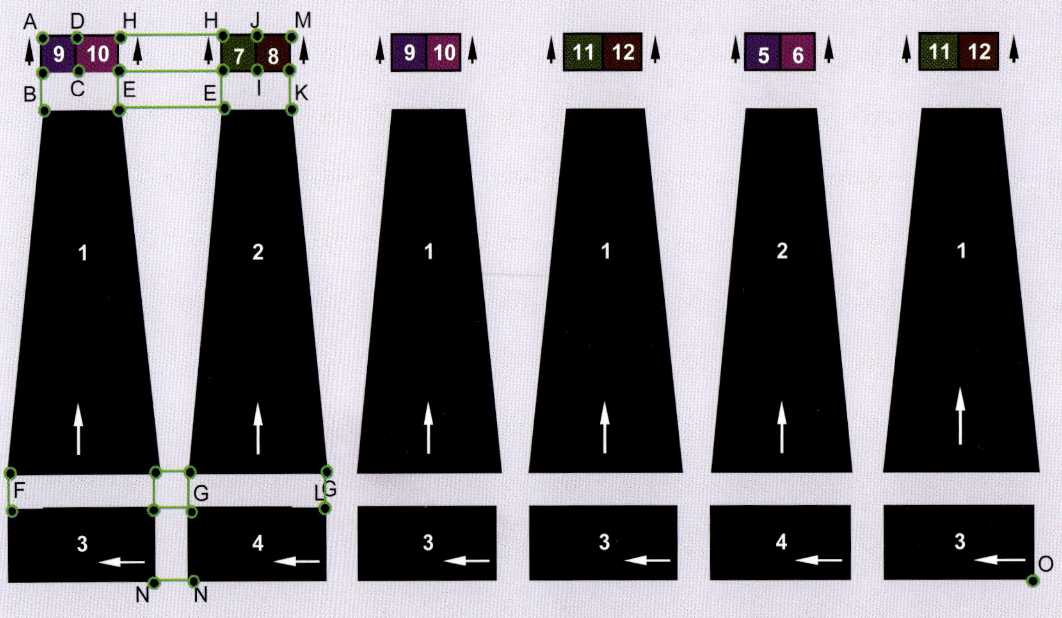

Softly Wrapped

Cuddle Up in this Oversized Jacket

Level of difficulty: Experienced
Size: Sm: 38/40 {M-Lg: 42/44}
Material: Wick yarn (46% merino wool, 28% bamboo, 12% cotton, 7% baby alpaca, 7% super kid mohair), or substitute any chunky yarn that knits to gauge; $1^3/_4$ oz (50g)/100m (110 yds per skein). Black: Sm: 10 skeins [$17^1/_2$ oz (500g), 1100 yds] {M-Lg: 11 skeins [19¼ oz (550g), 1210 yds]}; purple, pink, green, and brown: 1 skein each [$1^3/_4$ oz (50g); 110 yds, each]. 4 toggle closures.
Knitting needles: US 10 (6mm)
Crochet hook: US J/10 (6mm)
Basic pattern: Stockinette stitch
Stitch gauge: 12 stitches and 20 rows = 4" x 4" (10 cm x 10 cm)

1. Knitting the Individual Pieces

According to the table, knit 20 different individual pieces at the specified quantity = 49 pieces total. The number of stitches and rows, as well as the color and application of the pieces, are specified. Knit according to the general knitting chart for squares and rectangles (see page 6), except for the inner collar piece 15 and upper sleeve piece 16. Work these pieces according to the knitting charts 15 and 16 on page 18. Arrange the individual pieces according to the diagrams on page 20; arrows on the diagrams = working direction of the individual pieces.

2. Joining the Individual Pieces

Crochet together the individual pieces in black according to the general crochet diagram (see page 8) and the diagrams. The same points on the diagrams meet. Two pieces are always joined by preparation and closing (see pages 8 - 9), even if this is not always explicitly mentioned in the text.

		Holes		Cast On		Number of Rows		Stitches at the End to Cast Off			
Piece	Number	38/40	42/44	38/40	42/44	38/40	42/44	38/40	42/44	Color	Application
1	2	11 x 15	12 x 15	33	36	58	58	33	36	Black	Front piece
2	1	23 x 15	25 x 15	69	75	58	58	69	75	Black	Back piece
3	2	2 x 10	2 x 10	6	6	38	38	6	6	Brown	Waistband
4	4	2 x 10	2 x 10	6	6	38	38	6	6	Green	Waistband
5	4	2 x 10	2 x 10	6	6	38	38	6	6	Pink	Waistband
6	2	2 x 10	2 x 10	6	6	38	38	6	6	Purple	Waistband
7	2	2 x 10	3 x 10	6	9	38	38	6	9	Purple	Waistband
8	2	2 x 10	3 x 10	6	9	38	38	6	9	Brown	Waistband
9	2	11 x 10	12 x 10	33	36	38	38	33	36	Black	Underlay-Waistband / FP
10	1	10 x 23	10 x 25	30	30	90	98	30	30	Black	Underlay-Waistband / BP
11	4	2 x 14	2 x 14	6	6	54	54	6	6	Purple	Outer collar
12	4	2 x 14	2 x 14	6	6	54	54	6	6	Pink	Outer collar
13	3	2 x 14	2 x 14	6	6	54	54	6	6	Green	Outer collar
14	3	2 x 14	2 x 14	6	6	54	54	6	6	Brown	Outer collar
15	1	9 x 4 x 7	9 x 4 x 7	27	27	14	14	21	21	Black	Inner collar *
16	4	15 x 13 x 7	15 x 13 x 7	45	45	50	50	21	21	Black	Upper sleeve *
17	2	3 x 7	3 x 7	9	9	26	26	9	9	Green	Lower sleeve
18	2	3 x 7	3 x 7	9	9	26	26	9	9	Pink	Lower sleeve
19	2	3 x 7	3 x 7	9	9	26	26	9	9	Purple	Lower sleeve
20	2	3 x 7	3 x 7	9	9	26	26	9	9	Brown	Lower sleeve

* Worked according to the knitting chart

Joining the Front Pieces and Back Piece (Diagram 1)

Begin on the right front piece 1 at A: Prepare two edges over D to N; prepare a connecting single crochet stitch to O and piece 2 from O to D (= 1st armhole), connecting single crochet stitch to D on piece 1. Complete the first shoulder seam from D to C over 7 holes by preparation and closing. Prepare piece 2 over E and F to P; prepare connecting single crochet stitch to Q and piece 1 from Q to F (2nd armhole). Connecting single crochet stitch to F on piece 2, join the pieces 1 and 2 from F to E for the 2nd shoulder seam. Prepare the second piece 1 over H/I to J/R; then prepare the bottom edge over Q, P, O, and N to K.

Border and Underlay

Connect single crochet stitch to M at K. Join pieces 6, 5, 4, and 8 consecutively with piece 9, and, at the same time, with piece 1. For this, place piece 6 onto piece 9 with the wrong sides together; join both pieces together with piece 1 over 2 holes. Then, only prepare the long side of piece 6, and join piece 5 with piece 6. The crochet seam between piece 6 and 5 counts as 1 hole, therefore, after the last hole of piece 5, turn at the end of the crocheted junction. Prepare the 3rd hole of piece 9 alone and join on piece 1. Then join piece 5 and piece 9 together with piece 1 by preparation and closing. Proceed in this manner until the border pieces 4 and 8 + piece 9 are also joined together with piece 1. Join the border pieces 7, 5, 4, 3, 6, 5, 4, and 8 + piece 10 together with piece 2 in the same way. Then join the border pieces 7, 5, 4, and 3 + second piece 9 together with the second piece 10 to R/J. Lastly, combine the front piece edges of pieces 3 and 9, the bottom edge and the front piece edge of pieces 6 and 9 to M by preparation. Connecting single crochet stitch to K.

Collar and Outer Collar

Prepare the front piece edge from K to A. Work a connecting single crochet stitch to A on the collar piece 15 and join the collar edges from A over B and G to H with the neckline. Then prepare the edge from H to A; cut off the yarn. Double the outer collar pieces 11, 12, 13, and 14 in half with the wrong sides together, and instead of 14 holes each on the long edge, join together 7 doubled holes. Attach at T piece 12 and combine the 7 doubled holes to K by preparation.

Join piece 12 with piece 1; then combine the 2nd long side of piece 12 by preparation. Join the doubled piece 11 with piece 12. The crochet seam between piece 11 and 12 counts as 1 hole, subsequently directly join the following hole of piece 1 with the seam by preparation and closing. Then join piece 11 with piece 1. In this way, join all outer collar pieces over the points L/A to H/I to J with the front pieces and collar, combine the last doubled long edge of piece 11 to S by preparation. Lastly, work from S to T over the front piece edge, bottom edge, and 2nd front piece edge with reverse bobble stitches (see page 20). Cut off the yarn.

Working in the Sleeves (Diagram 2)

Newly attach at B piece 16: Join piece 16 with piece 1 from B to C; prepare the sleeve edge to E. Place the second piece 16 onto the first piece 16 and complete the sleeve seam to C by preparation and closing. Join the second piece 16 with piece 2 from C to B; then complete the second sleeve seam from B to F by preparation and closing.

Prepare the bottom sleeve edge from F all around, connecting single crochet stitch to G on piece 17. Join piece 17 with piece 16, prepare the long edge of piece 17. Join piece 18 with pieces 17 and 16. Prepare the long edge of piece 18. In this way, also join the pieces 19 and 20 with the sleeve edge and join with

Knitting Chart
Piece 15

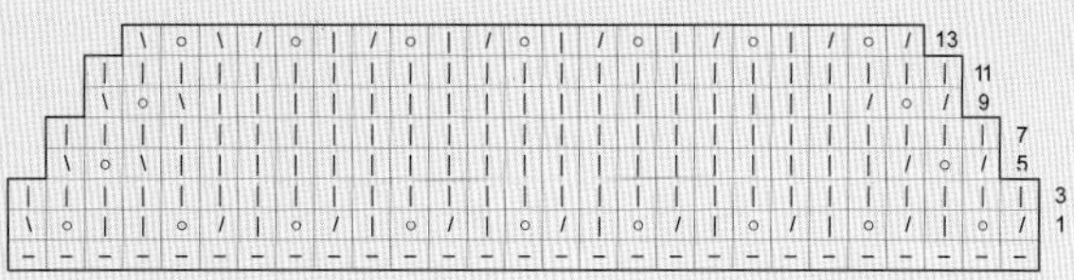

Knitting Chart
Piece 16

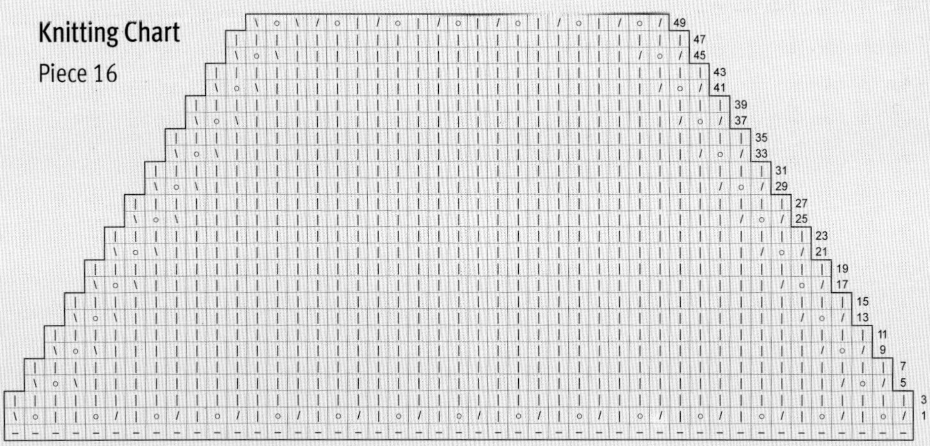

each other up to G. Prepare from G over H and I to H; then join pieces 17 and 20 from H to G. Cut off the yarn. Newly attach at H, and to finish, work a round of reverse bobble stitches as follows:

Work the **reverse bobble stitches** from left to right. Work a long reverse single crochet (= 1 single crochet stitch from left to right) in the center chain stitch of a cluster. (For the bobble, bring between 2 clusters of the edge finish around the chain stitch.) Draw 1 loop, 1 yarn over. (Repeat twice; then draw 1 more loop, and with 1 new yarn over, draw through all loops on the needle together. Then close the bobble with 1 chain stitch. Work a reverse single crochet around the following chain stitch, thereby the bobble is set to the right.) Always repeat after the last bobble end with 1 slip stitch in the 1st reverse single crochet.

Crochet on the 2nd sleeve inversely.

3. Finishing

Put three toggle closures evenly spread out on the right front piece through the holes of piece 6. Put the 4th closure through the last hole of piece 11. To close the collar, pull the other side of the closure through piece 5.

Diagram 1

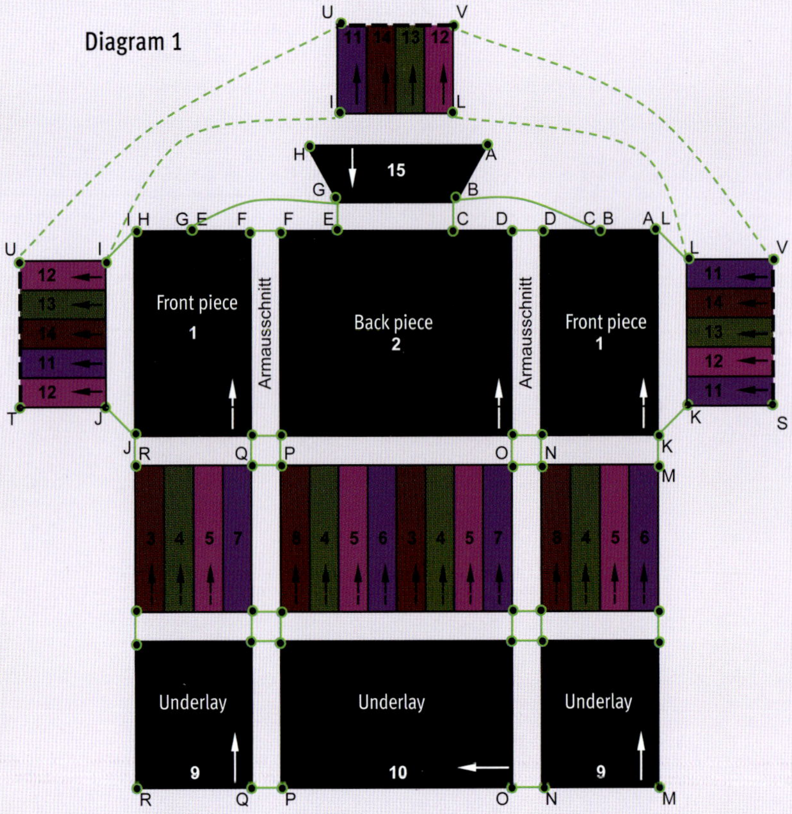

Diagram 2

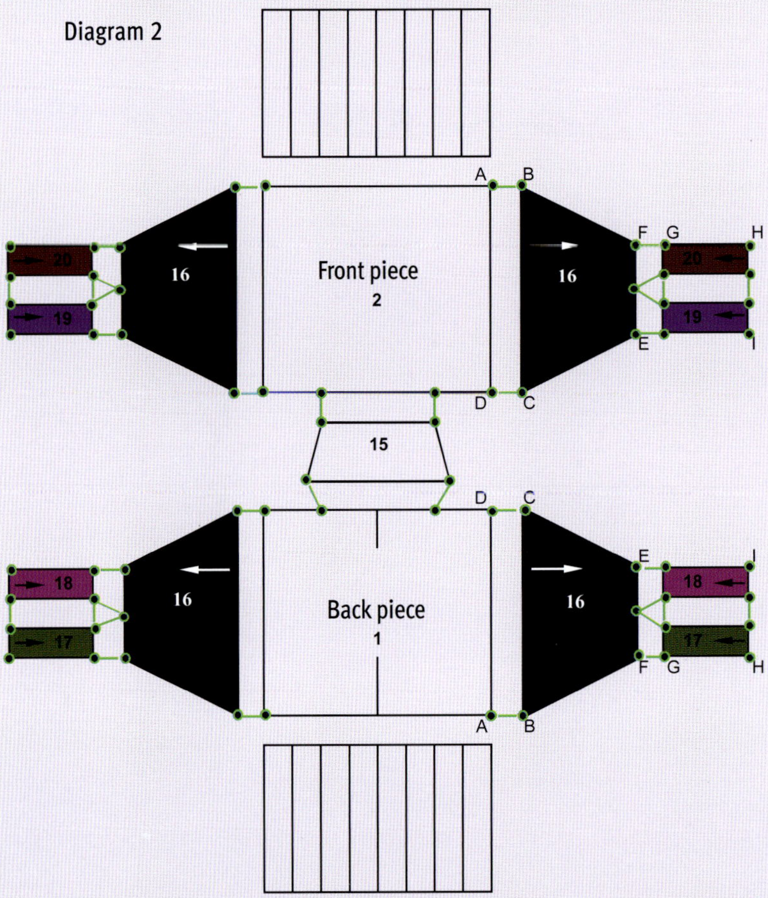

Colorfully Framed

Scarf with Pockets

Level of difficulty: Beginner
Size: One size fits all
Material: Wick yarn (46% merino wool, 28% bamboo, 12% cotton, 7% baby alpaca, 7% super kid mohair), or substitute any chunky yarn that knits to gauge; $1^3/_4$ oz (50g)/100m (110 yds per skein). Black: 4 skeins [7 oz (200g), 440 yds]; purple, pink, green, and brown: 1 skein each [$1^3/_4$ oz (50g), 110 yds, each]. 1 toggle closure.
Knitting needles: US 10 (6mm)
Crochet hook: US J/10 (6mm).
Basic pattern: Stockinette stitch
Stitch gauge: 12 stitches and 20 rows = 4" x 4" (10 cm x 10 cm)

1. Knitting the Individual Pieces

According to the table, knit 12 different individual pieces at the specified quantity = 32 pieces total. The number of stitches and rows, as well as the color and application of the pieces are specified. Knit according to the general knitting chart for squares and rectangles (see page 6). Arrange the individual pieces according to the diagram = working direction of the individual pieces.

2. Joining the Individual Pieces

Crochet together the individual pieces in black according to the general crochet diagram (see page 8) and the diagram on page 22. For the pockets, place two of piece 11 on top of each other with the wrong sides together and work doubled. Two pieces are always joined by preparation and closing (see pages 8 - 9), even if this is not always explicitly mentioned in the text.

Joining the Border and Trim

For the border, begin at A piece 1: Prepare the long edge to E, narrow edge, and second long edge. Join piece 2 with piece 1 by preparation and closing; prepare two edges of piece 2. Attach pieces 3, 4, and 5 consecutively like piece 2. Then prepare the narrow edge of piece 5 to point B.

For the trim, join piece 6 on a narrow edge with piece 5; prepare two edges of piece 6. Then also attach all trim pieces consecutively. For the second border, join piece 5 with piece 6 on a narrow edge; then prepare the long edge of piece 5 to C. Join piece 4 with piece 5; prepare the narrow and long edges of piece 4. Also attach the pieces 3, 2, and 1 consecutively. Finally, prepare the narrow edge of piece 1 to D.

Piece	Number	Holes	Cast on	Number of Rows	Color	Application
1	2	2 x 8	6	30	Brown	Border
2	2	2 x 8	6	30	Green	Border
3	2	2 x 8	6	30	Pink	Border
4	3	2 x 8	6	30	Purple	Border, Trim
5	2	2 x 8	6	30	Black	Border
6	4	2 x 4	6	14	Pink	Trim
7	4	2 x 4	6	14	Green	Trim
8	4	2 x 4	6	14	Brown	Trim
9	2	2 x 4	6	14	Purple	Trim
10	2	2 x 11	6	42	Black	Scarf
11	4	11 x 11	33	42	Black	Scarf
12	1	11 x 48	33	190	Black	Scarf

Joining the Scarf Pieces

Join piece 10 with pieces 1 to 4 by preparation and closing, work the junction to piece 6, and join with 2 holes of piece 6. Prepare the second long edge of piece 10. Double two of piece 11 (= pocket pieces) with the wrong sides together and join together first with piece 10, then with pieces 6, 7, and 8, combine the third edge of the doubled two of piece 11 by preparation. Join piece 12 with the doubled piece 11; then with the pieces 9 to 9 of the trim, prepare the second narrow edge of piece 12. Double two of piece 11 with the wrong sides together and join together first with piece 12, then with pieces 8, 7, and 6. Combine the third edge of the doubled two of piece 11 by preparation. Join piece 10 first with the doubled piece 11, then over 2 holes with piece 6, then with the pieces 4 to 1, end at E.

Edge Finish

Prepare the outer edge from E in black all around, combining the pocket pieces each over 6 holes up to the locations marked with "open" by preparation, at the open edges only prepare the bottom pocket piece, end at E. Work a round of reverse bobble stitches (see page 20) in black. Cut off the yarn. Newly attach on the pocket opening edges not yet crocheted, prepare the remaining 5 holes, and crochet over with reverse bobble stitches.

3. Finishing

Close the scarf with a toggle closure for a vest effect, by putting a toggle through the holes above the pocket pieces and turn.

Diagram

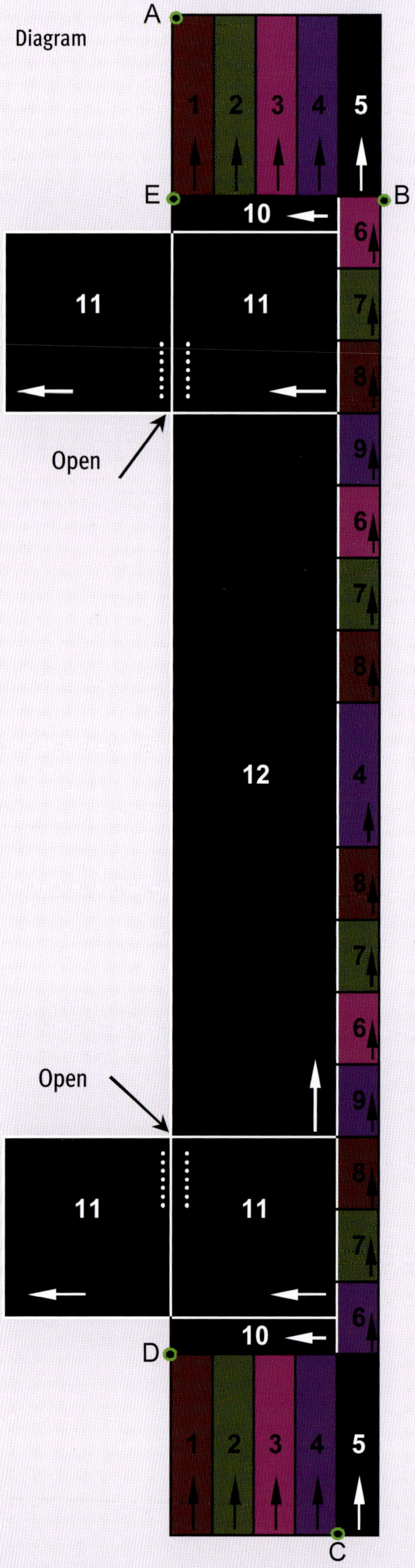

Warmly Recommended

Hat with a Colorful Border

Level of difficulty: Beginner
Size: 21 1/4" - 23 1/4" (54 cm - 59 cm) head circumference
Material: Wick yarn (46% merino wool, 28% bamboo, 12% cotton, 7% baby alpaca, 7% super kid mohair), or substitute any chunky yarn that knits to gauge; 1 3/4 oz (50g)/100m (110 yds per skein). Black: 2 skeins [3½ oz (100g), 220 yds]; purple, pink, green, and brown: 1 skein each [1 3/4 oz (50g), 110 yds, each]. 1 toggle closure.
Knitting needles: US 10 (6mm)
Crochet hook: US J/10 (6mm)
Basic pattern: Stockinette stitch
Stitch gauge: 12 stitches and 20 rows = 4" x 4" (10 cm x 10 cm)

1. Knitting the Individual Pieces

According to the table, knit 5 different individual pieces at the specified quantity = 11 pieces total. The number of stitches and rows, as well as the color and application of the pieces are specified. Knit according to the general knitting chart for squares and rectangles (see page 6); except head pieces 1 – Work these according to the adjacent knitting chart. Arrange the individual pieces according to the diagram.

2. Joining the Individual Pieces

Crochet together the individual pieces in black according to the general crochet diagram (see page 8) and the diagram. The same letters on the diagram meet. Two pieces are always joined by preparation and closing (see pages 8 - 9), even if this is not always explicitly mentioned in the text.

Joining the Head Pieces

Begin at A right piece 1: Prepare the edges over B and D to E, working two clusters in the tip at D. Join the second piece 1 with the first to D by preparation and closing; then prepare the second piece 1 to F. Join the third piece 1 with the second to D. Then join with the first piece 1 over B to A and join the head pieces to form a circle. Prepare the bottom border from A all around.

Joining the Border Pieces

Join piece 2 with piece 1 over 2 holes, then prepare the long edge to G. Join piece 3 first with piece 2, then with piece 1, then prepare the second long edge of piece 3. Proceed in this way until all border pieces are underneath each other and joined with the head pieces. Lastly prepare the long edge of the second piece 5 to C. Join the border to form a circle, for this join the first piece 2 with the second piece 5, end at A. Cut off the yarn.

Edge Finish

Newly attach in black at C and prepare the bottom border edge all around; end with 1 slip stitch in the 1st single crochet stitch. Then work 1 round of reverse bobble stitches (see page 20).

Knitting Chart
Piece 1

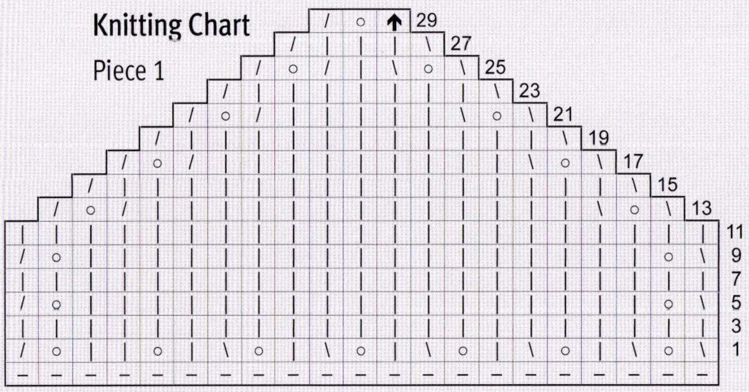

↑ = Slip 2 stitches together purlwise, knit 1 stitch, pull slipped stitches over it.

Piece	Number	Holes	Cast on	Rows	Color
1	3	7 x 8 x 1	21	30	Black *
2	2	2 x 4	6	14	Purple
3	2	2 x 4	6	14	Pink
4	2	2 x 4	6	14	Green
5	2	2 x 4	6	14	Brown

* Knitted according to the knitting chart

Diagram

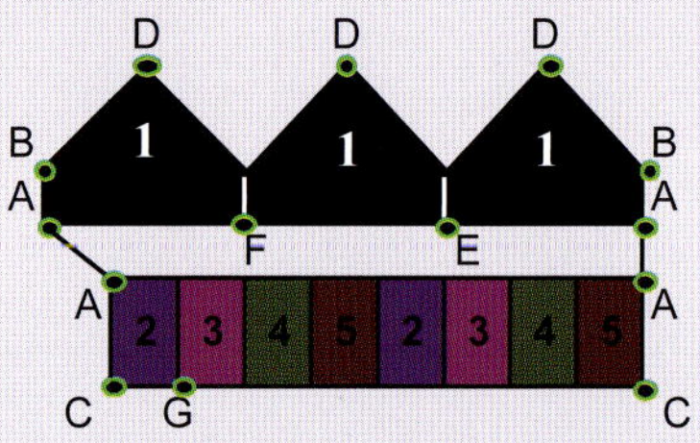

Cool on Hot Days

Top Made of Trendy Ribbon Yarn

Level of difficulty: Intermediate
Size: Sm: 36/38 {M: 40/42}
Material: Ribbon yarn (51% cotton, 49% polyacrylic), or substitute any heavy worsted yarn that knits to gauge; $1^{3}/_{4}$ oz (50g)/75m (82 yds per skein). White: Sm: 4 skeins [7 oz (200g), 328 yds] {M: 5 skeins [$8^{3}/_{4}$ oz (250g), 410 yds]}; pistachio, sky blue, aqua, and yellow: 1 skein each [$1^{3}/_{4}$ oz (50g), 82 yds, each].
Medium, worsted weight crochet cotton yarn (60% cotton, 40% polyacrylic; $1^{3}/_{4}$ oz (50g)/90m (99 yds per skein). White: Sm: 2 skeins [$3^{1}/_{2}$ oz (100g), 198 yds]; {M: 3 skeins [5 oz (150g), 297 yds]}
Knitting needles: US 7 (4.5mm)
Crochet hook: US G/6 (4mm)
Note: Work all individual pieces with ribbon yarn. Use the crochet yarn to join the pieces!
Basic pattern: Stockinette stitch
Double crochet stitch: According to the crochet diagram on page 28, work on the edge finish. Begin with 1 chain stitch and the stitches before the pattern repeat. Always repeat the pattern, at the same time, crocheting the double crochet stitch around the chain stitches of the edge finish, end with 1 slip stitch in the beginning chain stitch.
Stitch gauge: Ribbon yarn 15 stitches and 24 rows = 4" x 4" (10 cm x 10 cm)

1. Knitting the Individual Pieces

According to the table, knit 15 different individual pieces at the specified quantity = 31 pieces total. The number of stitches and rows and the color and application of the pieces are specified. Knit according to the general knitting chart for squares and rectangles (see page 6).

		Holes		Cast on		Number of rows		Color	Application
Piece	Number	36/38	40/42	36/38	40/42	36/38	40/42		
1	1	11 x 11	11 x 12	33	33	42	46	White	F
2	2	3 x 7	3 x 7	9	9	26	26	White	Side piece
3	2	3 x 11	3 x 12	9	9	42	46	White	F / B
4	1	15 x 11	15 x 12	45	45	42	46	White	B
5	1	3 x 11	4 x 11	9	12	42	42	White	F / B
6	1	3 x 3	3 x 3	9	9	10	10	Aqua	Side piece
7	2	3 x 3	3 x 3	9	9	10	10	White	Side piece
8	1	3 x 3	3 x 3	9	9	10	10	Sky blue	Side piece
9	2	3 x 3	3 x 3	9	9	10	10	Pistachio	F / B
10	2	3 x 3	3 x 3	9	9	10	10	Yellow	F / B
11	4	3 x 3	4 x 3	9	12	10	10	Sky blue	F / B
12	4	3 x 3	4 x 3	9	12	10	10	Aqua	F / B
13	4	3 x 3	4 x 3	9	12	10	10	Pistachio	F / B
14	2	3 x 3	4 x 3	9	12	10	10	Yellow	F / B
15	2	3 x 3	3 x 4	9	9	10	14	Pistachio	F / B

F = Front piece, B = Back piece

Arrange the individual pieces according to the diagram on page 28; arrows on the diagram = working direction of the individual pieces.

2. Joining the Individual Pieces

Crochet together the individual pieces with crochet yarn in white according to the general crochet diagram (see page 8) and the diagram. The same points on the diagram meet. Two pieces are always joined by preparation and closing (see pages 8 - 9), even if this is not always explicitly mentioned in the text.

Joining the Front, Back, and Side Pieces

Begin at A piece 7, first the wrong side is located at the front due to the direction of crocheting: Prepare three edges over B to C. Join piece 3 with piece 7 by preparation and closing; prepare 2 edges of piece 3 to D. Likewise attach piece 11 and piece 7 consecutively. Lastly, prepare an edge of piece 7 to F.

Join piece 8 with piece 7; prepare the following edge of piece 8. Join piece 12 first with piece 8; then with piece 11, prepare an edge of piece 12. Attach the pieces 9, 10, 15, and 6 in this way also, and at the same time, join with the pieces 3 and 7. Then prepare B over G to H.

Join piece 2 with piece 8; prepare the long edge of piece 2 to I. Join piece 12 over 3 holes with piece 2; then prepare an edge of piece 12. Join piece 11 with the pieces 12, 2, and

12; then prepare an edge of piece 11 and two edges of piece 12 to I.

Join piece 13 with piece 12; prepare an edge of piece 13. Join piece 1 on an edge consecutively with the pieces 13, 12, and 11. Join on the second edge with the pieces 9, 10, and 15; then prepare 7 holes on the third edge. Join piece 2 with the pieces 1 and 6 to G; then prepare the free edges of piece 2, 1, and 13 from G over E and J to the second J.

Join piece 14 with piece 13; prepare two edges of piece 14. Attach pieces 13, 13, 14, 13, 12, 11, 12, and 11 consecutively. Lastly, prepare an edge of piece 11 to D. Join piece 3 with piece 11; then prepare the long edge of piece 3 to B. Join piece 15 with piece 3; then prepare an edge of piece 15. Join piece 10 with the pieces 15 and 3; prepare an edge. Join piece 9 with the pieces 10, 3, and 12; then prepare the edges of pieces 9, 10, and 15 to G. Join piece 4 on an edge with the pieces 15, 10, and 9, and on the second edge with pieces 11, 12, 13, and 14; prepare the third edge to K.

Closing the Neckline

Join piece 5 with piece 4; prepare the long edge and join the second narrow edge to J with piece 1. Prepare the outer edges of pieces 5 and 4 (8 holes) from J to E.

Closing the Side Seams

Place the front and back pieces on top of each other and join the points E with a "connecting single crochet stitch." Complete the side seam over G, B to A by preparation and closing. Prepare the bottom edge from A to G = edge finish. Prepare the side edge and armhole from G over F, H, L, J, I to L. Join the points L of the front and back pieces with a "connecting single crochet stitch" and finish the second side seam over H, F to G by preparation and closing. Then prepare the bottom edge from G to A; end with 1 slip stitch in the 1st single crochet stitch at A = edge finish.

3. Finishing

From A crochet over the bottom edge with 1 round of double crochet stitches. Crochet over the neckline and armholes with a round of reverse single crochets (single crochet stitches from left to right).

Crochet Diagram

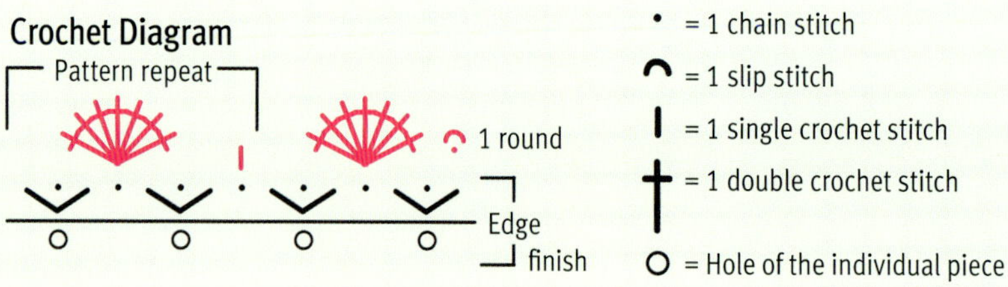

Diagram

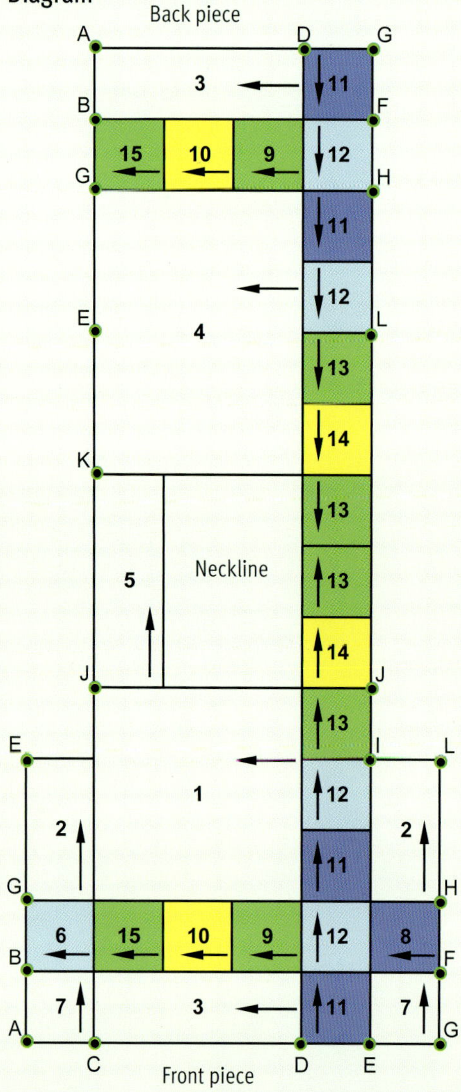

Chic Sun Protection

Hat for a Stylish Vacation Outfit

Level of difficulty: Beginner

Size: 21¼" - 23¼" (54 cm - 59 cm) head circumference

Material: Ribbon yarn (51% cotton, 49% polyacrylic), or substitute any heavy worsted yarn that knits to gauge; 1¾ oz (50g)/75m (82 yds per skein). White, pistachio, aqua, and yellow: 1 skein each [1¾ oz (50g), 82 yds, each]. Medium, worsted weight crochet cotton yarn (60% cotton, 40% polyacrylic; [1¾ oz (50g)/90m (99 yds per skein). White: 2 skeins [3½ oz (100g), 198 yds].

Knitting needles: US 7 (4.5mm)

Crochet hook: US G/6 (4mm)

Note: Work all individual pieces with ribbon yarn. Use the crochet yarn to join the pieces and for the finishing edge!

Basic pattern: Stockinette stitch

Stitch gauge: ribbon yarn 15 stitches and 24 rows = 4" x 4" (10 cm x 10 cm)

1. Knitting the Individual Pieces

According to the table, knit 4 different individual pieces at the specified quantity = 13 pieces total. The number of stitches and rows, as well as the color and application of the pieces are specified. Knit according to the general knitting chart for squares and rectangles (see page 6). Arrange the individual pieces according to the diagram; arrows on the diagram = working direction of the individual pieces.

2. Joining the Individual Pieces

Crochet together the individual pieces with crochet yarn according to the general crochet diagram (see page 8) and the diagram below. The same points on the diagram meet. Two pieces are always joined by preparation and closing (see pages 8 - 9), even if this is not always explicitly mentioned in the text.

Diagram

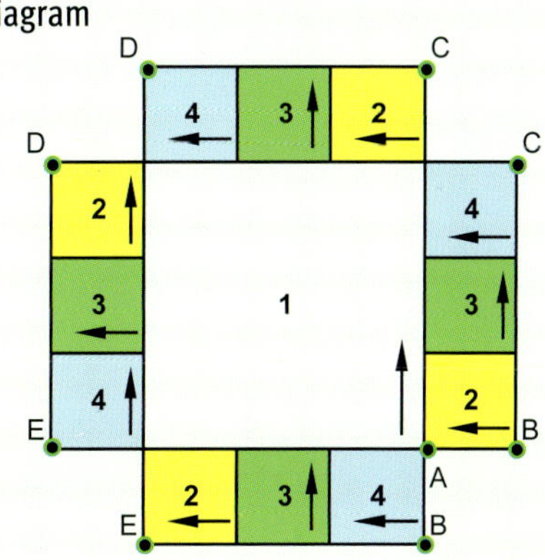

Begin at A piece 1: Prepare piece 1 all around, working 2 clusters each in the corner holes. Join piece 2 from A with piece 1 on an edge by preparation and closing; prepare the second edge of piece 2. Join piece 3 first with piece 2, then with piece 1; prepare the third edge of piece 3. Attach all following side pieces consecutively like piece 3; to close the row join the last piece 4 also with the first piece 2 on an edge, end at B. Prepare the bottom border of the hat from B; end after the last chain stitch with 1 slip stitch in the 1st single crochet stitch = edge finish.

Piece	Number	Holes	Cast on	Number of rows	Color	Application
1	1	9 x 9	18	34	White	Head Piece
2	4	2 x 2	6	6	Yellow	Side Piece
3	4	2 x 2	6	6	Pistachio	Side Piece
4	4	2 x 2	6	6	Aqua	Side Piece

3. Finishing

Continue crocheting for the finishing edge from B as follows: **1st round** – Proceed with 3 slip stitches to the chain stitch between 2 clusters of the edge finish; 3 chain stitches count as the 1st double crochet stitch and 1 double crochet stitch around the chain stitch, (with 1 chain stitch skip 3 stitches of the edge finish, 2 double crochet stitches around the following chain stitch, from) * always repeat, end with 1 chain stitch and 1 slip stitch in the 3rd beginning chain stitch. **2nd round** – Proceed with 2 slip stitches to the following chain stitch of the preceding round, (2 single crochet stitches around the chain stitch, with 1 chain stitch skip 2 stitches of the preceding round, from) * always repeat, end with 1 slip stitch in the 1st single crochet stitch. **3rd round** – Proceed with 2 slip stitches to the following chain stitch of the preceding round, then crochet like the 2nd round. **4th round** – Crochet reverse single crochets (= single crochet stitches from left to right).

Summer Hit in White

Shrug with an Eyecatching Crochet Flower Inset

Level of difficulty: Intermediate

Size: $57^{1}/_{2}$" (146 cm) long

Material: Ribbon yarn (51% cotton, 49% polyacrylic), or substitute any heavy worsted yarn that knits to gauge; $1^{3}/_{4}$ oz (50g)/75m (82 yds per skein). White: 8 skeins [14 oz (400g), 656 yds].

Medium, worsted weight crochet cotton yarn (60% cotton, 40% polyacrylic; [$1^{3}/_{4}$ oz (50g)/90m (99 yds per skein). White: 3 skeins [5¼ oz (150g), 297 yds].

Knitting needles: US 7 (4mm)

Crochet hook: US G/6 (4mm).

Note: Work the individual piece with ribbon yarn, the granny squares with crochet yarn. Use crochet yarn for joining and the reverse bobble stitches.

Basic pattern: Stockinette stitch

Granny square: Chain 5; join with slip stitch to form a ring. According to the crochet diagram, crochet 3 rounds – the 1st and 3rd rounds begin with 1 chain stitch and end with 1 slip stitch in the beginning chain stitch. The 2nd round begins with 1 long loop for the 1st puff stitch and ends with 1 double crochet stitch in the head of the 1st puff stitch. Work all following granny squares like the first; however, in the 3rd round, join 3 times on one side with the previous square. For this, after the puff stitch, work 1 single crochet stitch in the corresponding puff stitch of the previous square on the corners (arrows A and E); in the side center (arrow C), substitute the middle chain stitch of the chain space by 1 single crochet stitch around the chain space of the previous square.

Stitch gauge: Basic pattern 15 stitches and 24 rows = 4" x 4" (10 cm x 10 cm); granny square = $3^{3}/_{8}$" x $3^{3}/_{8}$" (8.5 cm x 8.5 cm)

1. Knitting/Crocheting the Pieces

According to the table, knit 1 individual piece. The number of stitches and rows is specified. Knit according to the general knitting chart for squares and rectangles (see page 6).

Additionally, work 12 granny squares, in the process joining these into 2 strips of 6 squares each.

Arrange the individual piece and granny square strips according to the diagram; arrow on the diagram = working direction of the individual piece.

Piece	Number	Holes	Cast on	Number of rows
1	1	20 x 88	60	350

2. Joining Together the Pieces

Crochet together the individual piece and the granny square strips with crochet yarn according to the general crochet diagram (see page 8) and the diagram on page 31. The same points on the diagram meet.

Note: Do not prepare the granny square strips before joining. Instead, work as follows: Work the 1st connecting single crochet stitch in the head of the corner puff stitch marked with arrow A. Work the following 3 connecting single crochet stitches each after a cluster around the chain space marked with the arrows B to D, and work the 5th connecting single crochet stitch in the head of the corner puff stitch marked with arrow E. Thus, each granny square is joined with the individual piece over 5 holes.

Begin at point A piece 1: Prepare piece 1 from A to H; at the same time, join over 30 holes with the first granny square strip as described. Then prepare the edge over 28 holes from H to G; subsequently, prepare the edge from G to B. At the same time, join with the 2nd granny square strip over 30 holes. Prepare the narrow strip from B to C. Prepare the 2nd long edge of piece 1, and at the same time, join with the bottom side of the granny square strip from C to D and from E to F, only preparing in between from D to E. Lastly, prepare the narrow edge from F to A.

3. Finishing

Crochet around the inner part as well as the sleeve edges with 1 round of reverse bobble stitches (see page 20).

Crochet Diagram

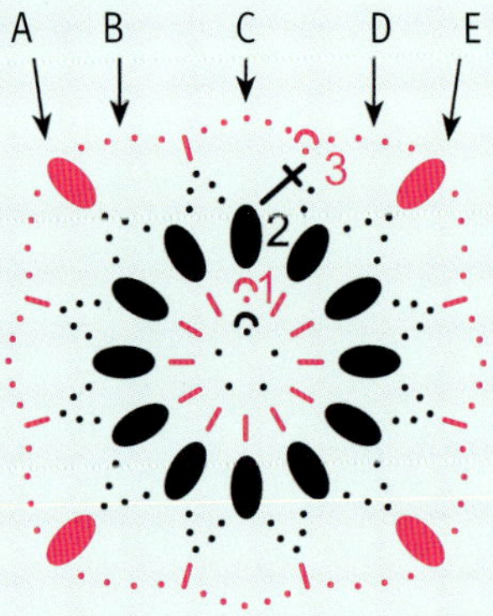

= 1 chain stitch
= 1 slip stitch
= 1 single crochet stitch
= 1 double crochet stitch

= 1 puff stitch: * Insert into the stitch or around the chain space of the preceding round, draw and pull up 1 loop and, 1 yarn over. * Repeat 3 more times; then draw through together all loops on the needle and work 1 chain stitch for closing the bobble.

Diagram

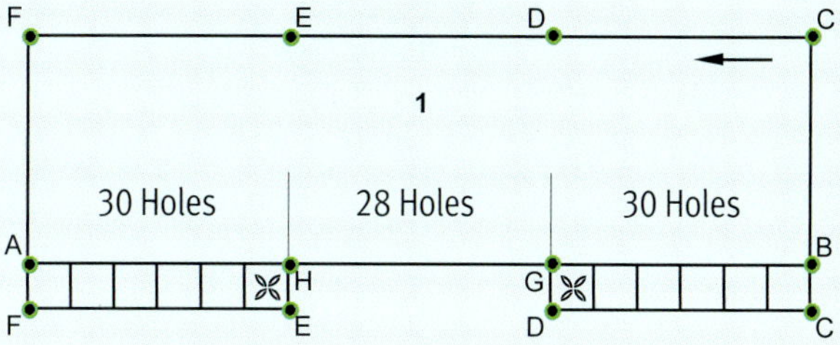

Favorite Fleece Piece

Flattering Poncho in Soft Pastel Tones

Level of difficulty: Beginner
Size: 36 - 44
Material: Fleece yarn (56% polyamide, 44% polyacrylic); about 3/4 oz (25g)/51m (56 yds per skein). Lilac: 14 skeins [about 12 3/4 oz (350g), 784 yds]; purple and aubergine: 5 skeins each [about 3 1/2 oz (100g), 224 yds, each]; turquoise: 2 skeins [about 1½ oz (50g), 112 yds].
Knitting needles: US 10 (6mm)
Crochet hook: US H/8 (5mm)
Basic pattern: Stockinette stitch
Stitch gauge: 14 stitches and 20 rows - 4" x 4" (10 cm x 10 cm)

1. Knitting the Individual Pieces

According to the table, knit 10 different individual pieces at the specified quantity = 48 pieces total. The number of stitches and rows, as well as the color are specified. Knit according to the general knitting chart for squares and rectangles (see page 6).

Arrange the individual pieces according to the diagram; arrows on the diagram = working direction of the individual pieces.

2. Joining the Individual Pieces

Crochet together the individual pieces in lilac according to the general crochet diagram (see page 8) and the diagram on page 34.

Two pieces are always joined by preparation and closing (see pages 8 - 9), even if this is not always explicitly mentioned in the text.

Joining the Left Front Sleeve and Front Piece

Begin at A piece 4: Prepare three edges over B, C to D. Join piece 1 with piece 4 to C by preparation and closing; prepare to E. Join piece 2 with the pieces 1 and 4 to B; prepare two edges over F to G. Join piece 5 with piece 2 from G to F; prepare two edges over H to I. Join piece 10 with piece 5 to J; prepare the long edge of piece 10. Join piece 6 with piece 10; then prepare the narrow edge to L. Join piece 4 first with piece 6, then with piece 10 to J. Lastly, join with piece 5 to H. Prepare pieces 4 and 6 over L to M; then prepare the narrow edges of the pieces 6 and 10. Join piece 2 with the pieces 10 and 6 to M. Prepare the free edges of pieces 2 and 10 from M over P, Q to I.

Join piece 9 with the pieces 10 and 2 from I to Q; then prepare three edges over U and K to I, then subsequently prepare piece 5 to G.

Attaching the Finishing Border

Join piece 4 with the pieces 5 and 9 by preparation and closing; then prepare the second narrow edge. Join the border pieces 7, 3, 8, 3 (junction at K, see page 9), 7, and 4 also with the preceding piece and join with piece 9 to U. Lastly, prepare the narrow edge of piece 4 to T. Cut off the yarn.

Joining the Right Front Sleeve and Front Piece

Newly attach at Q piece 2: Join pieces 2 and piece 9 by preparation and closing; prepare the long edge of piece 2. Join piece 6 with piece 2 over 3 holes, then prepare 2 edges of piece 6. Join piece 4 with piece 6, then prepare the long edge of piece 4. Join piece 10 consecutively with the pieces 4, 6, 2, and 9 to U, then prepare pieces 10 and 4 from U to R. Join piece 5 from R to U with the pieces 4 and 10, then join with piece 4 from U to T, then prepare the second long edge of piece 5. Join piece 2 with piece 5. Prepare two edges of piece 2 from T over S to V. Join piece 4 with piece 2 over 3 holes, then prepare the long edge of piece 4. Join piece 1 first with piece 4, then with piece 2 to S. Cut off the yarn.

Piece	Number	Holes	Cast on	Number of rows	Color
1	4	7 x 7	21	26	Lilac
2	8	3 x 11	9	42	Purple
3	4	3 x 7	9	26	Purple
4	12	3 x 7	9	26	Turquoise
5	4	3 x 11	9	42	Aubergine
6	4	3 x 7	9	26	Aubergine
7	4	3 x 3	9	10	Aubergine
8	2	3 x 3	3	10	Lilac
9	2	19 x 19	57	74	Lilac
10	4	7 x 15	21	58	Lilac

Edge Finish

Attach yarn at Q; prepare the neckline and sleeve edges over R, V, S to T, the edge of the finishing border to G, and the sleeve edges over W to A. The front poncho piece is finished.

Likewise work the back poncho piece, however, when working the right back sleeve and the edge finish, join together both poncho pieces on the shoulder sleeve edges and on the bottom "sleeve seams" by preparation and closing.

3. Finishing

Crochet around the neckline and bottom sleeve edges, as well as the border edges, with a round of reverse single crochets (= single crochet stitch from left to right) in lilac.

Diagram

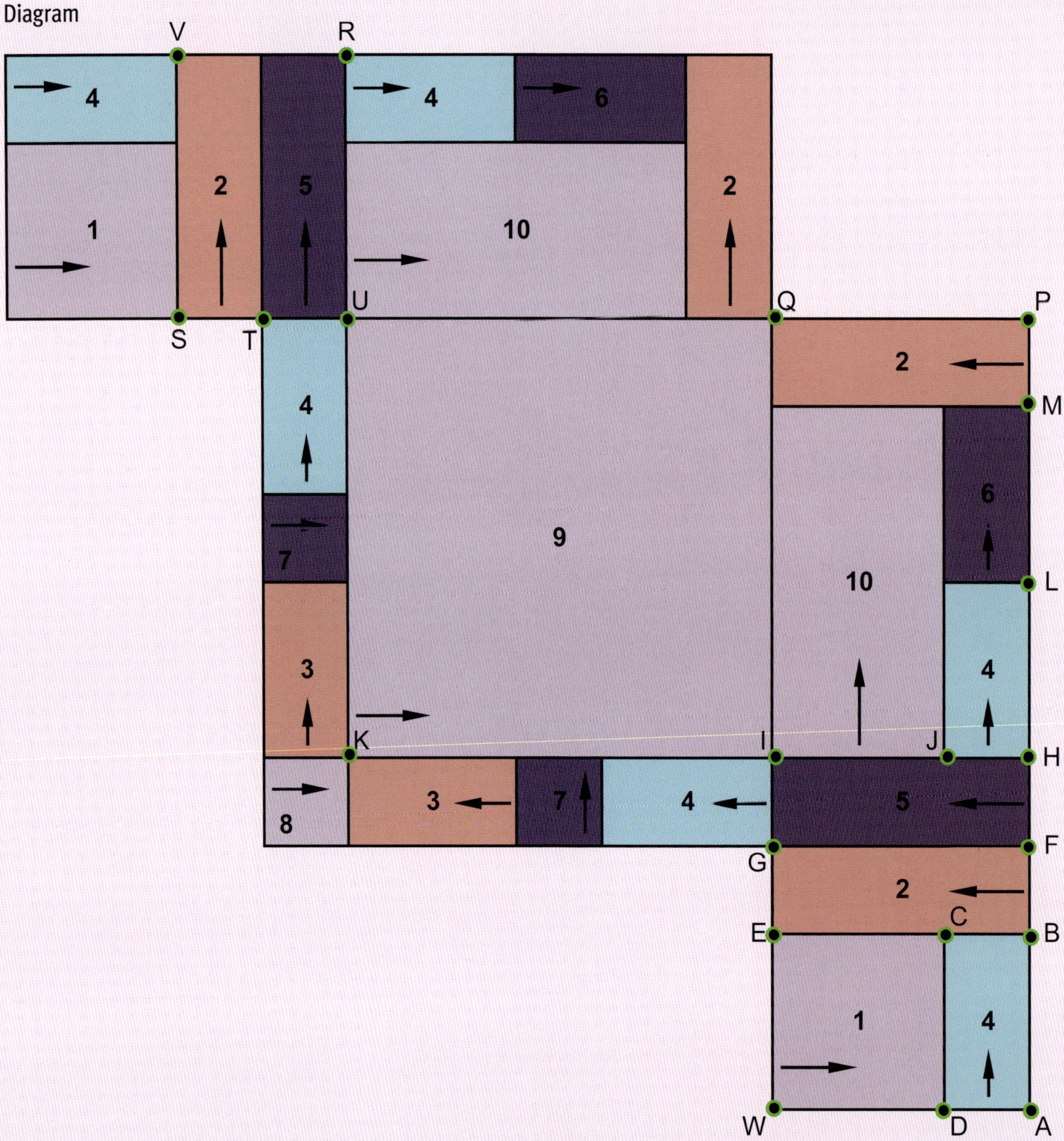

Quick-Change Artist

A Jacket – A Wearable Art Vest: Two Looks in One

Level of difficulty: Intermediate
Size: Sm: 36/38 {M: 40/42; Lg: 44/46}
Material: Sport yarn (100% superwash virgin wool); $1^3/_4$ oz (50g)/125m (137 yds per skein). Multicolor: Sm: 10 skeins [$17^1/_2$ oz (500g), 1370 yds] {M: 11 skeins [$19^1/_2$ oz (550g), 1507 yds]; Lg: 12 skeins [21 oz (600g), 1644 yds]}; rust: Sm: 3 skeins [$5^1/_4$ oz (150g), 411 yds] {M: 3 skeins [$5^1/_4$ oz (150g), 411 yds]; Lg: 4 skeins [7 oz (200g), 548 yds]}. 16 buttons and 4 toggle closures.
Knitting needles: US 3 (3mm)
Crochet hook: D/3 (3-3.25mm)
Basic pattern: Stockinette stitch
Stitch gauge: 24 stitches and 36 rows = 4" x 4" (10 x 10 cm)

1. Knitting the Individual Pieces

According to the table, knit 13 different individual pieces at the specified quantity = 50 pieces total. The number of stitches and rows, as well as the color and application, are specified. Knit according to the general knitting chart for squares and rectangles (see page 6), except for sleeve piece 13 – work this according to the knitting chart, in the process repeating the pattern 13 times.

Arrange the individual pieces according to the diagrams on pages 38 and 40; arrows on the diagrams = working direction of the individual pieces.

Knitting Chart
Piece 13

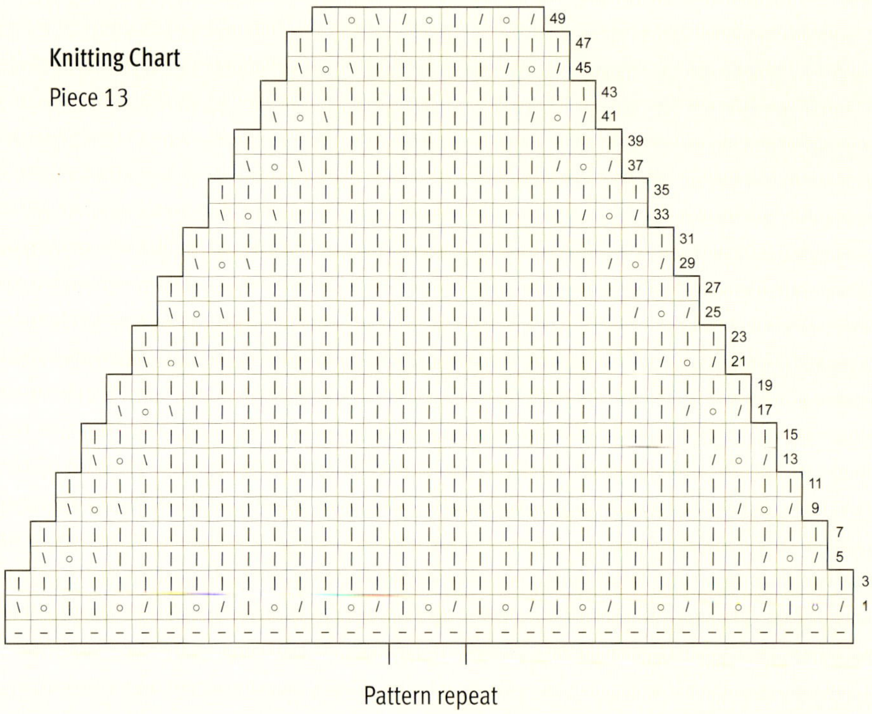

		Holes			Cast on			Number of rows				
Piece	Number	36/38	40/42	44/46	36/38	40/42	44/46	36/38	40/42	44/46	Color	Application
1	14	7 x 7	7 x 7	7 x 7	21	21	21	26	26	26	Multicolored	Plaid/Sleeve
2	5	7 x 7	9 x 7	11 x 7	21	27	33	26	26	26	Multicolored	Plaid
3	4	7 x 7	7 x 9	7 x 11	21	21	21	26	34	42	Multicolored	Plaid
4	3	7 x 15	7 x 15	7 x 15	21	21	21	58	58	58	Multicolored	Plaid
5	3	15 x 15	15 x 15	15 x 15	45	45	45	58	58	58	Multicolored	Plaid
6	2	15 x 15	15 x 17	15 x 19	45	45	45	58	66	74	Multicolored	Plaid
7	3	7 x 15	9 x 15	11 x 15	21	27	33	58	58	58	Multicolored	Plaid
8	1	23 x 23	25 x 23	27 x 23	69	75	81	90	90	90	Multicolored	Plaid
9	2	23 x 23	23 x 25	23 x 27	69	69	69	90	98	106	Multicolored	Plaid
10	1	31 x 31	35 x 31	39 x 31	93	105	117	122	122	122	Multicolored	Plaid
11	4	7 x 23	7 x 23	7 x 23	21	21	21	90	90	90	Multicolored	Sleeve
12	4	7 x 23	7 x 23	7 x 23	21	21	21	90	90	90	Rust	Sleeve
13	4	23 x 13 x 15	23 x 13 x 15	23 x 13 x 15	69	69	69	50	50	50	Rust	Sleeve

2nd Side Piece (Diagram 1)

Begin at T piece 6: Join piece 6 with piece 10 to U; prepare two edges. Join piece 4 with piece 6, prepare an edge to V. Join the first piece 1 with piece 4; prepare an edge. Join the second piece 1 with the first, and with piece 6, prepare an edge. Join piece 2 with the pieces 1 and 6, only prepare the third edge for the armhole and the following bottom edge. Join piece 9 with the pieces 1, 1, and 2, only prepare the following edge for the armhole over 15 holes; join the remaining edge with the center piece edge to R, prepare the third edge. Join the pieces 1, 1, and 3 with both pieces 9 (for the sequence see the pieces 1, 1, 2 as before); prepare the bottom edge of the pieces. Then likewise attach the pieces 5 and 7; end at S. Prepare the remaining outer edges over V, T, N, M, and J to A.

Diagram 2

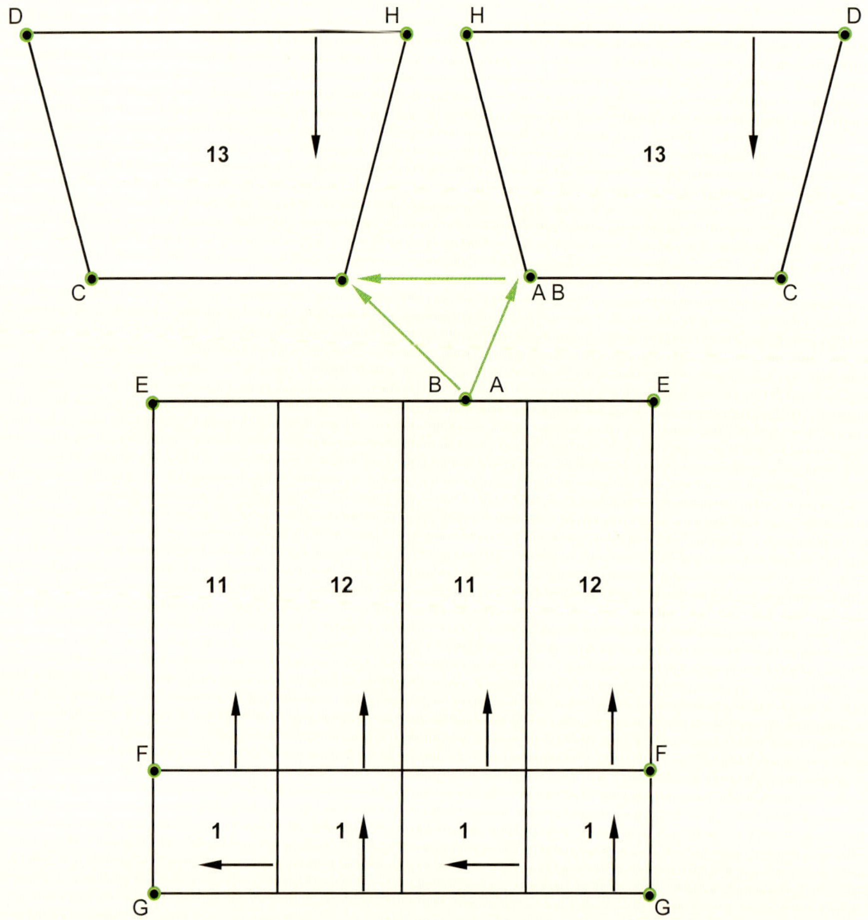

Joining the Sleeves (Diagram 2):

Begin at G piece 1 on the left side of the bottom sleeve: Prepare three edges of piece 1 to F. Join piece 11 with piece 1; prepare the long edge. Join piece 12 with piece 11; prepare the narrow edge. Join piece 1 with the pieces 12 and 1; then prepare the bottom edge and long edge of piece 1 + 12. Likewise, attach the following pieces 11 + 1 and 12 + 1, and prepare the outer edges from G over F, E to E. Double the sleeves in half and complete the sleeve seam from E to G by preparation and closing. Cut off the yarn.

Attach yarn at A piece 11 on the bottom sleeve; junction from A (3rd hole piece 11) to A piece 13 on the top sleeve. From A to C join the first piece 13 with the pieces 11 (3 holes), 12, and 11 (3 holes). Prepare an edge piece 13 from C to D; then for the sleeve seam, join both pieces 13 from D to C. T-junction to piece 11 (4th hole) and further join pieces 11 (3 holes), 12, and 11 (3 holes) with piece 13 to B. Work the junction from B to A and A. For the second sleeve seam, join both pieces 13 from B to H. Lastly, prepare the top border all around.

3. Finishing

For the edge, finish crochet around the plaid from A in rust as follows: **1st round** – Proceed with 3 slip stitches to the following chain stitch between two clusters; 3 chain stitches count as the 1st double crochet stitch and 1 double crochet stitch around the chain stitch (with 1 chain stitch skip 3 stitches of the edge finish, 2 double crochet stitches around the following chain stitch), always repeat, end with 1 chain stitch and 1 slip stitch in the 3rd beginning chain stitch. **2nd round** – Proceed with 2 slip stitches to the following chain stitch (2 single crochet stitches around the chain stitches, with 1 chain stitch skip 2 stitches of the preceding round), always repeat, end with 1 slip stitch in the 1st single crochet stitch. **3rd round** – Crochet reverse single crochets (= single crochet stitches from left to right). Likewise, crochet around the top and bottom sleeve edges. Crochet around the arm holes on the plaid in rust with a round of reverse single crochets. For buttoning on the sleeves, sew on 8 buttons, each evenly distributed on the armholes of the plaid. The double crochet stitch clusters of the edge finish on the top sleeve serve as button holes. To close the jacket / vest, put 3 toggle closures through the double crochet stitch clusters of the plaid and turn according to Diagram 1. Place the fourth closure on the shoulder. The collar is closed with it.

Casual City Look

Pullover with Feminine Charm

Level of difficulty: Medium
Size: Sm: 36/38 {M: 40/42; Lg: 44/46}
Material: Ribbon yarn (51% cotton, 49% polyacrylic), or substitute any heavy worsted yarn that knits to gauge; 1 3/4 oz (50g)/75m (82 yds per skein). Coral: Sm: 6 skeins [10 1/2 oz (300g), 492 yds] {M: 7 skeins, [12 ¼ oz (350g), 574 yds]; Lg: 8 skeins [14 oz (400g), 656 yds]}.
Worsted weight crochet yarn (60% cotton, 40% polyacrylic; 1 3/4 oz (50g)/90m (99 yds per skein). Lobster: Sm: 2 skeins [3 1/2 oz (100g), 198 yds] {M: 3 skeins [5 oz (150g), 297 yds]; Lg: 3 skeins [5 oz (150g), 297 yds]}; olive, primrose, and lemon: 1 skein each [1 3/4 oz (50g), 99 yds, each].
Knitting needles: US 7 (4.5mm
Crochet hook: US G6, 4mm
Basic pattern: Stockinette stitch
Stitch gauge: With ribbon yarn 15 stitches and 24 rows = 4" x 4" (10 cm x 10 cm); with crochet yarn 16 stitches and 26 rows = 4" x 4" (10 cm x 10 cm)

1. Knitting the Individual Pieces

According to the table, knit 9 different individual pieces at the specified quantity with ribbon yarn (pieces 1 to 6) and crochet yarn (pieces 7 to 9) = 24 pieces total. The number of stitches and rows, as well as the color and application of the pieces, are specified. Knit according to the general knitting chart for squares and rectangles (see page 6), except for sleeve piece 6 – work this according to the knitting chart on page 44, at the same time working the pattern repeat for all sizes 5 times.
Arrange the individual pieces according to the diagram on page 45, placing all pieces 2 and 4 with the reverse stockinette outward (see "Li" on the diagram); arrows on the diagram = working direction of the individual pieces.

2. Joining the Individual Pieces

Crochet together the individual pieces in with crochet yarn lobster according to the general crochet diagram (see page 8) and the diagram. The same points in the diagram meet. Two pieces are always joined by preparation and closing (see pages 8 9), even if this is not always mentioned explicitly in the text.

Joining the Front and Back Piece

Begin on the right front piece side at I piece 1: Prepare two edges over C to B. Join piece 9 from B to C with piece 1 by preparation and closing; prepare two edges of piece 9 over E to D. Join the second piece 9 with the first from D to E (= shoulder seam), then prepare two edges over G to F. Join piece 4 with piece 9 from F to G; prepare the long edge from piece 4 from G to H. Join piece 5 with piece 4 to J, then prepare piece 5 to U. Join piece 8 with piece 5; prepare the second edge of piece 8. Join piece 7 with piece 8, then with piece 5; prepare the third edge of piece 7. Likewise, attach the following pieces 7 and 8, joining the second piece 8 from J to G with piece 4 also. Prepare the neckline edge of pieces 8, 7, 7 and 8 to S; then prepare the following edges of pieces 8 and 5 to T. Join the second piece 4 with the pieces 5 and 8 to S; prepare the narrow side to R. Join piece 9 with piece 4 to S; prepare over E to D.
Join the last piece 9 with the previous piece 9 to E (= shoulder seam), prepare two edges over R to Q. Join piece 1 with piece 9 to R; prepare the long edge to Z. Join piece 2 with piece 1 to P, prepare from P to O. Join piece 8 with the pieces 2 and 1 from O over P to R; then prepare two edges of piece 8 and the long edge of piece 2 to Q. Join piece 3 with

		Holes			Cast on			Number of rows			Material/ Color	Application
Piece	Number	36/38	40/42	44/46	36/38	40/42	44/46	36/38	40/42	44/46		
1	2	3 x 27	4 x 27	5 x 27	9	12	15	106	106	106	Coral	F Side
2	2	3 x 23	3 x 23	3 x 23	9	9	9	90	90	90	Coral	Front piece
3	1	7 x 19	7 x 19	7 x 19	21	21	21	74	74	74	Coral	Front piece
4	2	3 x 27	4 x 27	5 x 27	9	12	15	106	106	106	Coral	RT side
5	1	15 x 23	15 x 23	15 x 23	45	45	45	90	90	90	Coral	Back Side
6	4	15 x 13 x 7	15 x 13 x 7	15 x 13 x 7	45	45	45	50	50	50	Coral	Sleeve
7	4	3 x 3	3 x 3	3 x 3	9	9	9	10	10	10	Primrose	F + B
8	4	3 x 3	3 x 3	3 x 3	9	9	9	10	10	10	Lemon	F + B
9	4	3 x 3	4 x 3	5 x 3	9	12	15	10	10	10	Olive	F + B

Knitting Chart
Piece 6

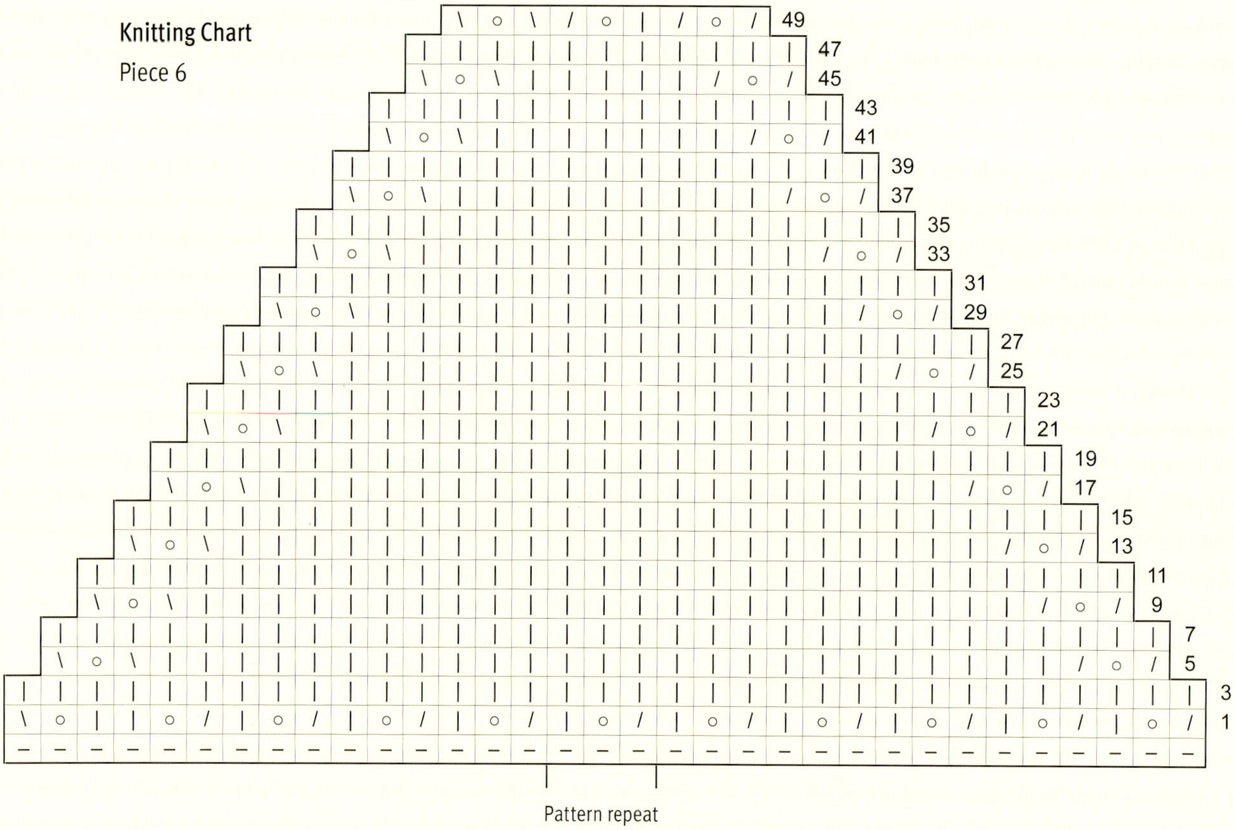

piece 2 from Q to N; prepare the narrow edge to M. Join both pieces 7 from M to N with piece 3, at the same time not working a crochet junction between the pieces 7 for the slot – instead, skip the cluster of the center hole of piece 3 with slip stitches = bottom slot edge. Join the second piece 7 from N to O with piece 2. Prepare both pieces 7 on the free edges to K, thereby crocheting over the slot edges (red lines) of pieces 7 separately and cast on with 1 connecting single crochet stitch on the bottom slot edge before turning. Then prepare the edges of pieces 7 and 3 from K over M to L. Join piece 2 with the pieces 3 and 7 from L over M to K; prepare the narrow edge to J. Join piece 8 with piece 2 from J to K; then prepare two edges to C. Work 1 connecting single crochet stitch to piece 1 and join the pieces 8 and 2 with piece 1 to I. Cut off the yarn.

Closing the Side Seams and Working in the Sleeves

Attach at A on the front piece; prepare piece 1 and 9 to D. Work a connecting single crochet stitch to piece 6 and join piece 6 with the pieces 9 and 1 from D to W; prepare 3 edges over X and Y to D. Put on the second piece 6 with the right sides together. Join the edges of both pieces from D to Y = top sleeve seam. Prepare the second piece 6 from Y to X, then join the edges from X to W = bottom sleeve seam. Lastly, prepare the edge from W to D on the second piece 6. Work the junction for the first piece 6 and the second piece 9 (back piece). Join the sleeve piece from D to W with the pieces 9 and 4; then complete the side seam from W to A by preparation and closing. Prepare the bottom back side edge from A to V = edge finish.

Attach the left sleeve inversely; end with the edge finish of the front piece from V to A and 1 slip stitch in the 1st single crochet stitch at A.

3. Finishing

Continue crocheting for the hem from A in lobster as follows: **1st round** – Proceed with slip stitches to the following chain stitch between two clusters; 3 chain stitches count as the 1st double crochet stitch and 1 double crochet stitch around the chain stitch (with 1 chain stitch skip 3 stitches of the edge finish [= 1 single crochet stitch + 1 chain stitch + 1 single crochet stitch], 2 double crochet stitches around the following chain stitch). Always repeat, end with 1 chain stitch and 1 slip stitch in the 3rd beginning chain stitch. **2nd round** – Proceed with 2 slip stitches to the following chain stitch of the preceding round (2 single crochet stitches around the chain stitch;

with 1 chain stitch, skip 2 stitches of the preceding round). Always repeat, end with 1 slip stitch in the 1st single crochet stitch. **3rd round** – Proceed with 2 slip stitches to the following chain stitch of the preceding round, then crochet like the 2nd round. 4th round – Crochet reverse single crochets (= single crochet stitches from left to right). Likewise, crochet around the bottom sleeve edges. Crochet around the neckline and the slot edges from E with 1 round of reverse single crochets in lobster.

Diagram

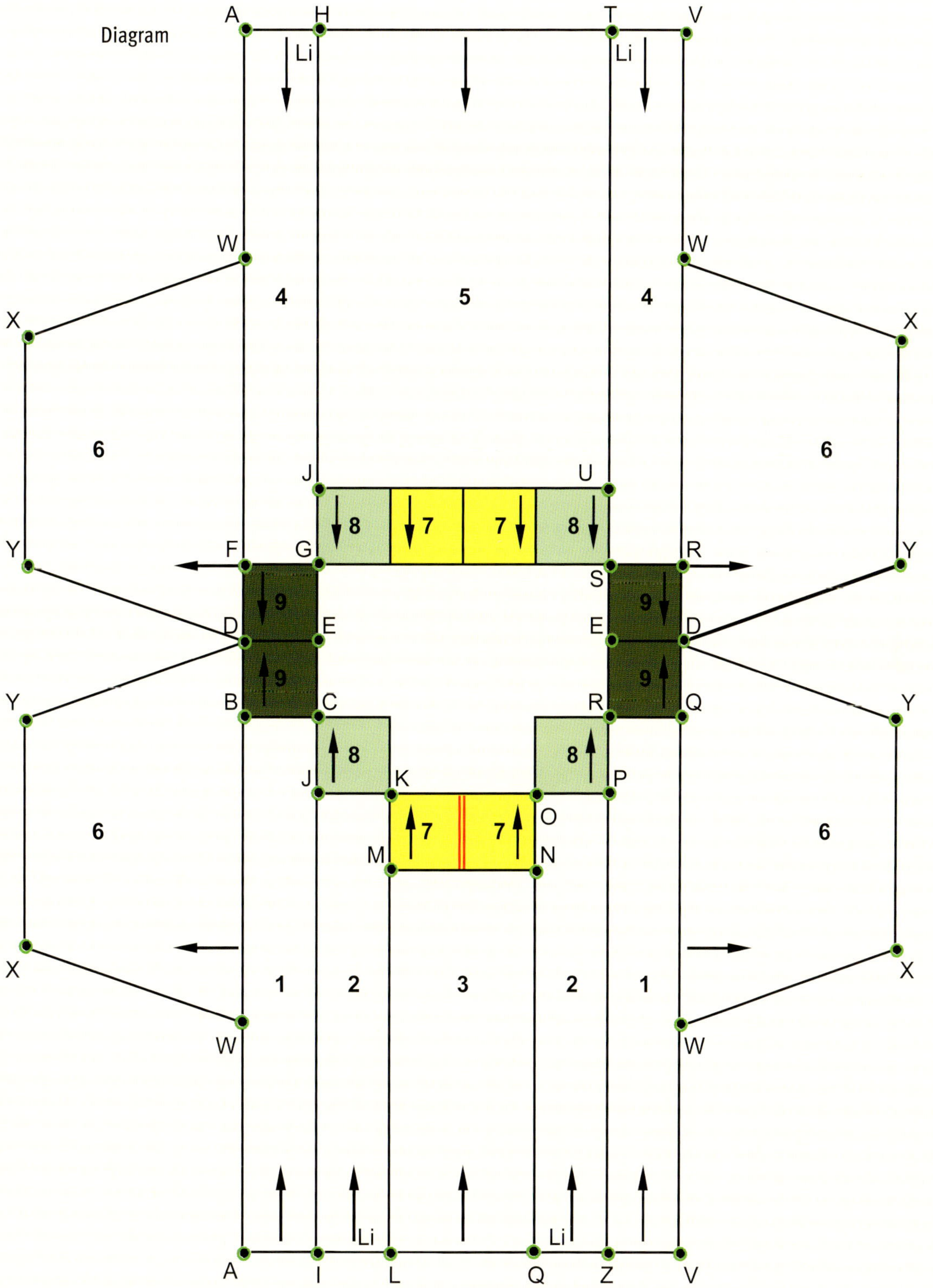

Eyecatcher In Red

Plaid Jacket with Detachable Sleeves

Level of difficulty: Intermediate
Size: 38-44
Material: Chunky weight weight yarn (40% virgin wool, 33% polyacrylic, 27% polyamide), or substitute any chunky yarn that knits to gauge; 1 3/4 oz (50g)/130m (143 yds per skein). Red: 12 skeins [21 oz (600g), 1760 yds]. Black: [3 1/2 oz (100g), 286 yds].
Decorative ribbon (41% virgin wool, 36% polyacrylic, 9% viscose, 4% polyester), 1 3/4 oz (50g)/15m (33 yds per skein). Red: 2 skeins [3 1/2 oz (100g), 66 yds]. 16 buttons.
Knitting needles: US 10 (6mm)
Crochet hook: US H/8, 5mm.
Note: Knit the individual pieces with wool yarn and crochet together. Use the decorative ribbon as edging.
Basic pattern: Stockinette stitch
Stitch gauge: 14 stitches and 20 rows = 4" x 4" (10 cm x 10 cm)

1. Knitting the Individual Pieces

According to the table, knit 6 different individual pieces with wool yarn at the specified quantity = 41 pieces total. The number of stitches and rows, as well as the color and application, are specified. Knit according to the general knitting chart for squares and rectangles (see page 6). Arrange the individual pieces according to the diagrams on pages 48 and 49. Arrange the pieces marked on the diagrams with the addition "Li" with the back side = reverse stockinette outward; arrange all remaining pieces with the front side = stockinette outward. Arrows on the diagrams = working direction of the individual pieces.

2. Joining the Individual Pieces

Crochet together the individual pieces with wool yarn in red according to the general crochet diagram (see page 8) and the diagrams 1 to 3. The same points on the diagram meet.
During the work step preparation, incorporate the decorative ribbon as edging along the thick red lines on the diagrams as follows: Place the decorative ribbon with the top edge over the holes of the piece not yet prepared; then with the crochet hook, take through the decorative ribbon and the hole during preparation so that the top edge of the decorative ribbon is included. Carry along the ribbon so loosely that a ruche effect forms. The opposite side, with which subsequently will be joined, does not get edging.
Two pieces are always joined by preparation and closing (see pages 8 - 9), even if this is not always explicitly mentioned in the text.

Plaid (Diagram 1)

1st Side Piece

Begin at A piece 1: Prepare two edges over B to C. Join the first piece 1 with the second from C to B; prepare two edges of the second piece 1 over D to E. Join the third piece 1 with the second from E to D; prepare two edges of the third piece 1 over Q to F, and prepare all edges of the pieces 1 over E and C to G. Join pieces 1 and 3 from G to C; prepare the long edge of piece 3 to H. Join piece 5 with piece 3 and the pieces 1 from H over C and E to F; prepare pieces 5 and 3 from F over I and H to J. Likewise, attach the following block made out of three pieces 1, piece 5 and 3. Lastly, prepare the long edge of piece 3 to Z.

Center Piece

Join piece 6 with piece 3 over 8 holes from Z to K; then for the armhole (red double line), prepare 11 holes of piece 6 alone. Join piece 6 again with piece 1 to I at the remaining 3 holes; prepare the following edges of piece 6 over N to M. Join piece 1 with piece 6 to N; then prepare two edges of piece 1. Join the following piece 1 with the previous one; then prepare an edge to O. Join piece 5 with the pieces 1, 6, and 5 over N, I to F; prepare the bottom edge of pieces 5 and 1 to P. Join the third piece 1 with the second piece 1 from P to O; prepare an edge of piece 1. Join piece 3 with the pieces 1, 5, and 1 over O, F to Q. Prepare all edges from Q over X, P, M, and R to L.

Piece	Number	Holes	Cast on	Number of rows	Color	Application
1	21	7 x 7	21	26	Red	Plaid/Sleeve
2	4	7 x 7	21	26	Black	Sleeve
3	7	7 x 15	21	58	Red	Plaid/Sleeve
4	1	7 x 15	21	58	Black	Sleeve
5	7	15 x 15	45	58	Red	Plaid/Sleeve
6	1	23 x 23	69	90	Red	Plaid

2nd Side Piece

Join piece 1 with piece 6 from L to R; prepare the following edge to S. Join both pieces 1 from S to R; prepare two edges of the second piece 1 to U – an opening for the armhole remains (red double line). Join two of piece 1 up to the armhole, then prepare 2 holes alone, from the 4th connecting single crochet stitch join piece 1 with piece 6 to M. Prepare the pieces 1 from M over U and S to T. Join piece 3 with the top piece 1 to S; prepare the long edge to V. Join piece 5 with piece 3 and over U with two of piece 1; prepare the following edge to W. Correspondingly, attach the last block, end at X. Prepare the remaining outer edges of X on the 2nd side piece over the top edge up to A on the 1st side piece.

Left Sleeve (Diagram 2)

Begin on the left side at A piece 1: Prepare two edges of piece 1 over E to F. Join piece 2 with piece 1 to E; prepare two edges of piece 2. Join another piece 2 with the first to G; then prepare up to A and further over B to B on the left side.

Likewise, attach the pieces 2, 1, and 1 of the second row to B; then prepare the two edges over C on the right side to C on the left side.

Join piece 3 with piece 2; prepare the long edge to H. Join piece 5 with piece 3 and two of piece 1 to C on the right side; prepare from C over D and H to D. Double the sleeves with the wrong sides together; the same letters meet. Work 1 connecting single crochet stitch from D to D and complete the sleeve seam to A by preparation and closing.

Right Sleeve (Diagram 3)

Begin on the left side at A piece 2: Prepare three edges from A over E and F to B. Join piece 1 with piece 2; prepare an edge to G. Join piece 4 with the pieces 1 and 2 over F to E; prepare the narrow and long edges over I to H. Join the top piece 1 with piece 4, prepare the second edge to B. Join the second piece 1 with the first and with piece 4 to I. Then prepare the edges of the pieces 1, 1, 4, and 1 from I over A, B, C, H, and G to C.

Join piece 3 with piece 1 to G; prepare the long edge to J. Join piece 5 with piece 3 to G and with the pieces 4 and 1 from G over H to C.

Prepare the edge to D, then further prepare from D over J to D. Double the sleeves with the wrong sides together; the same letters meet. Work 1 connecting single crochet stitch from D to D and complete the sleeve seam to A by preparation and closing.

Diagram 1

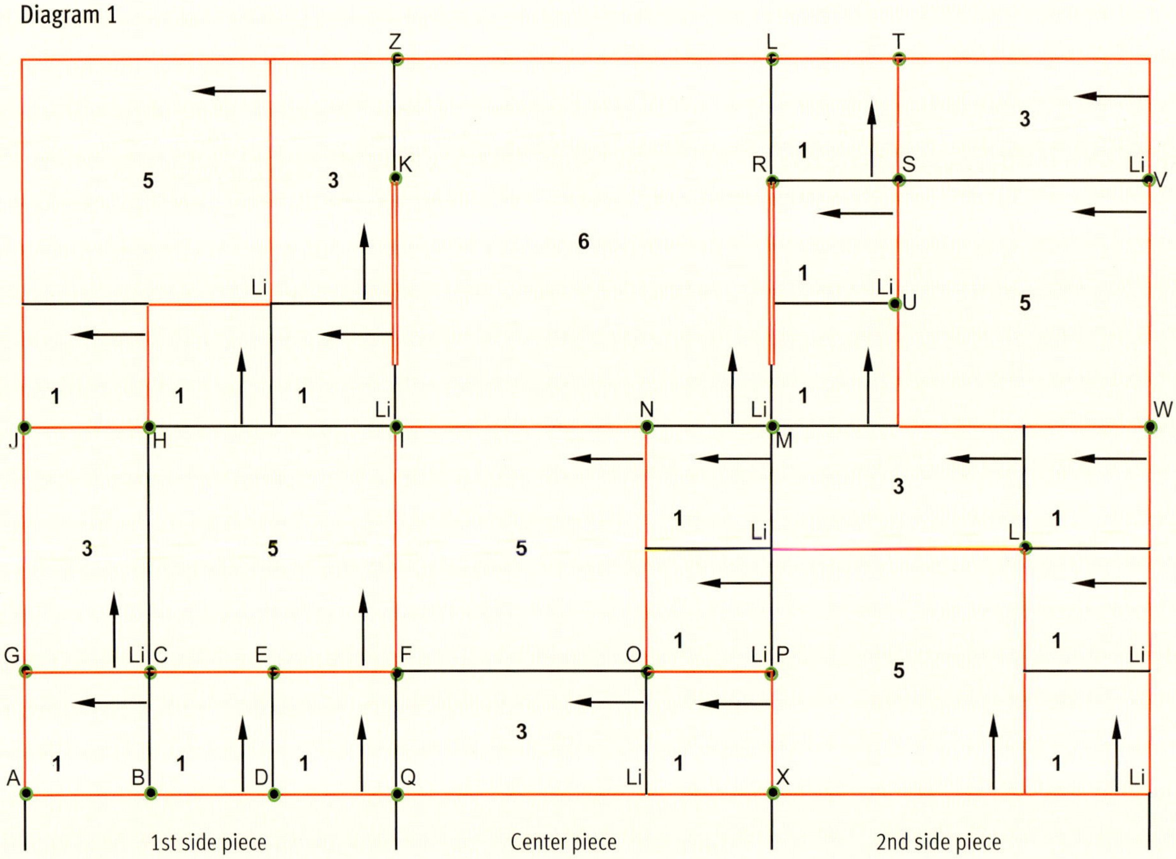

= sleeve opening over 11 holes per side (pieces are not joined)

3. Finishing

On the outer edges of the plaid and on the bottom sleeve edges crochet an edge finish out of wool yarn in red, in the process working this as with preparation and include the decorative ribbon. However, work the clusters offset between the clusters of the edge that is already prepared. Crochet around the armhole on the plaid from K and R with a round of reverse single crochets (= single crochet stitches from left to right) out of wool yarn in red. Crochet around the top sleeve edges as follows: Attach the yarn on the sleeve seam, proceed with 3 slip stitches to the following chain stitch between two clusters, work 3 chain stitches count as the 1st double crochet stitch and 1 double crochet stitch around the chain stitch of the preceding round (with 1 chain stitch skip 2 stitches of the edge finish, 2 double crochet stitches around the following chain stitch). Always repeat, end with 1 slip stitch in the 3rd beginning chain stitch. To finish, crochet 1 round of reverse single crochets. For buttoning on the sleeves, sew on 8 buttons evenly distributed on the armhole edges of the plaid. The double crochet stitch clusters on the top sleeve border serve as button holes. To close the jacket, use the buttons of the sleeves. For this, button the buttons on the left shoulder edge through the crochet edge of the right front piece. In case that is not sufficient, additionally pull a toggle closure through the holes of both front pieces and turn.

Diagram 2 (Left Sleeve)

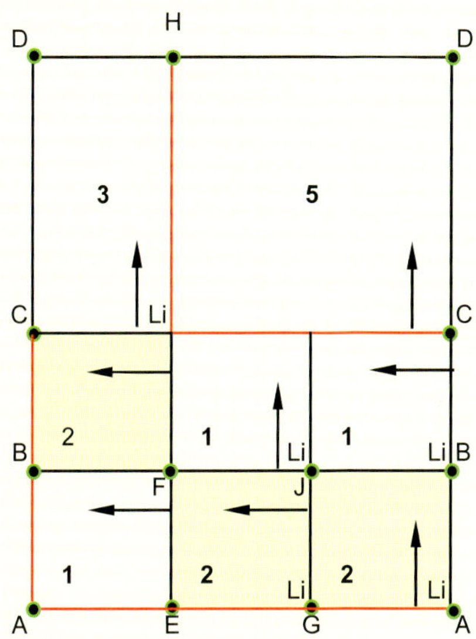

Diagram 3 (Right Sleeve)

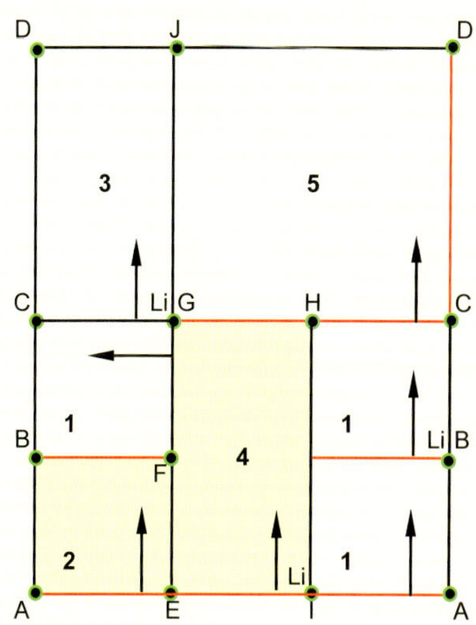

Perfect Companion

Scarf with Pockets

Level of difficulty: Beginner

Size: One size fits all

Material: Chunky weight yarn (40% virgin wool, 33% polyacrylic, 27% polyamide); 1 3/4 oz (50g)/130m (143 yds per skein). Black: 4 skeins [7 oz (200g), 572 yds]. Red: 1 skein [1 3/4 oz (50g), 143 yds].

Decorative ribbon (41% virgin wool, 36% polyacrylic, 9% viscose, 4% polyester); 1 3/4 oz (50g)/15m (16 yds per skein). Black: 1 skein [1 3/4 oz (50g), 16 yds]. 1 button.

Knitting needles: US 10 (6mm)

Crochet hook: US H8 (5mm)

Note: Work the individual pieces with yarn and crochet together with yarn. Use the ribbon as edging.

Basic pattern: Stockinette stitch

Stitch gauge: 14 stitches and 20 rows = 4" x 4" (10 cm x 10 cm)

1. Knitting the Individual Pieces

According to the table, knit 6 different individual pieces at the specified quantity = 10 pieces total. The number of stitches and rows, as well as the color and application are specified. Knit according to the general knitting chart for squares and rectangles (see page 6).

Arrange the individual pieces according to the diagram. Arrange the pieces on the diagram marked with the addition "Li" with the back side = reverse stockinette outward; arrange all remaining pieces with the front side = stockinette outward. Arrows on the diagram = working direction of the individual pieces.

2. Joining the Individual Pieces

Crochet together the individual pieces with wool yarn in black according to the general crochet diagram (see page 8) and the diagram. Two pieces are always joined by preparation and closing (see pages 8 - 9), even if this is not always explicitly mentioned in the text. At the locations on the diagram marked with red, incorporate the decorative ribbon as edging during the work step preparation: Place the decorative ribbon with the top edge over the holes of the piece not yet prepared; then with the crochet hook, take through the decorative ribbon and hole during preparation so that the top edge of the decorative ribbon will be included. Carry along the ribbon loosely so that a ruche effect forms. The opposite side, with which subsequently will be joined, does not get edging.

Begin at A piece 3: Prepare an edge from A to B. Prepare piece 2 from B to C with piece 3. Prepare an edge to D. Join the second piece 2 with the first from D to C; prepare two edges over A to E. The joined pieces 3, 2, and 2 form the top side of the pocket. Place this with the inside on the reverse stockinette of the underlay piece 5 (the same letters E, A, and I meet)

Piece	Number	Holes	Cast on	Number of rows	Color	Application
1	1	7 x 7	21	26	Red	Top Pocket
2	3	7 x 7	21	26	Black	Top Pocket
3	2	7 x 15	21	58	Black	Top Pocket
4	1	7 x 15	21	58	Red	Scarf Piece
5	2	15 x 15	45	58	Black	Underlay
6	1	15 x 50	45	198	Black	Scarf Piece

Diagram

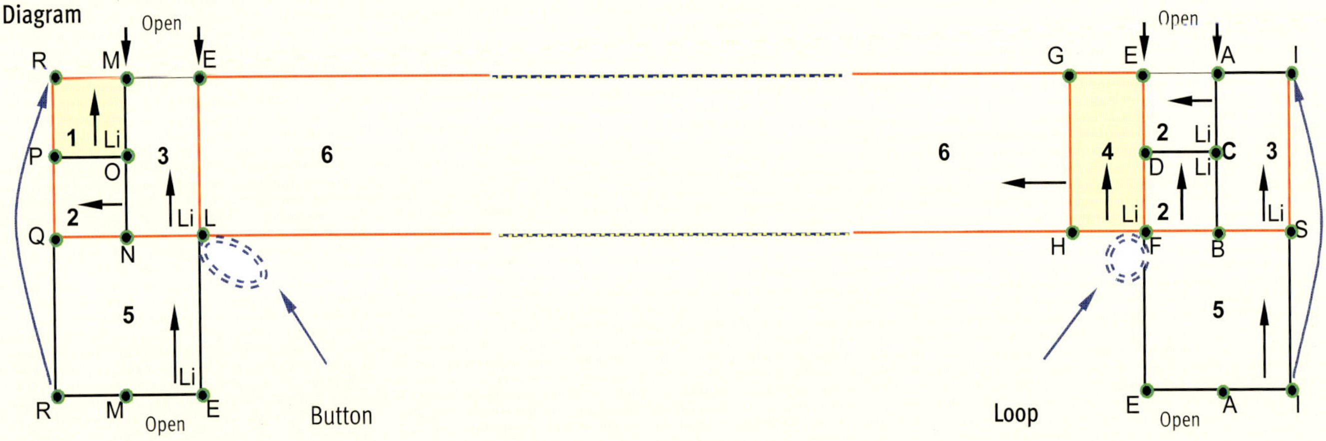

and work both pieces together as a pocket as follows. First, combine the edges of both pieces from E to F by preparation. Then join the pocket with piece 4 to E; prepare two edges over G to H. Join piece 4 with piece 6 from H to G; prepare piece 6 over E to L. Place piece 3 with the stockinette on the stockinette of the underlay piece 5 and join both pieces together with piece 6 to E, then prepare two edges of piece 3 over M to N alone. Join piece 3 with piece 2 to O; prepare piece 2 to P. Join piece 1 with the pieces 2 and 3 over O to M. Cut off the yarn.

Newly attach the yarn at E piece 3 left side. Prepare the pocket underlay of piece 5 to M over 7 holes alone (pocket opening). From the 8th hole, combine the edges of piece 5 and the pieces 1, 2, and 3 over R, P, Q, and N to L by preparation (the same letters E, M, and R meet). Prepare the outer edge piece 6 and 4 over H to F. Combine pocket edges of piece 5 with the pieces 2 and 3 over B, S, and I to A by preparation. Prepare the pocket underlay of piece 5 to E over 7 holes alone (pocket opening). Cut off the yarn.

3. Finishing

According to the diagram, at L crochet chain stitches in black on a loop at the size of the button; then crochet around the chain stitch tightly with single crochet stitches. Sew on the button at F according to the diagram.

Slim Silhouette

Pullover with Stripes

Level of difficulty: Intermediate
Size: Sm: 36/38 {M: 40/42; Lg: 44/46}
Material: Sport weight yarn (100% superwash virgin wool); 1 3/4 oz (50g)/125m (137 yds per skein). Brown and natural: Sm: 4 skeins each [7 oz (200g), 548 yds, each] {M: 5 skeins each [9 oz (250g), 685 yds, each]; Lg: 6 skeins each [10 1/2 oz (300g), 822 yds, each]}.
Knitting needles: US 6 (4mm)
Crochet hook: US G/6 (4mm)
Basic pattern: Stockinette stitch
Stitch gauge: 26 stitches and 32 rows = 4" x 4" (10 cm x 10 cm)

1. Knitting the Individual Pieces

According to the table, knit 11 different individual pieces at the specified quantity = 28 pieces total. The number of stitches and rows, as well as the color and application of the pieces, are specified. Knit according to the general knitting chart for squares and rectangles (see page 6), except for sleeve piece 11 – work this according to the knitting chart on page 54, working the pattern repeat 13 times.

Arrange the individual pieces according to the diagram on page 55; arrows on the diagram = working direction of the individual pieces.

2. Joining the Individual Pieces

Crochet together the individual pieces according to the general crochet diagram (see page 8). The same points on the diagram meet. Two pieces are always joined by preparation and closing (see pages 8 - 9), even if this is not always explicitly mentioned in the text.

Joining the Front Piece

Begin on the shoulder edge of the front piece at point I piece 2: Prepare three edges of piece 2 over A and C to B. Join piece 7 with piece 2 on a long edge by preparation and closing; prepare the narrow edge piece 7. Join piece 6 first with piece 7, then with piece 2; prepare the narrow edge of piece 6. Join piece 8 with the pieces 6 and 2; prepare the narrow edge of piece 8 to D. Prepare the free long edges of pieces 8, 6, and 7 to E. Join piece 1 with the pieces 7, 6, and 8 to D on a long edge; then prepare the narrow edge and the following long edge of piece 1. Attach all remaining strips for the front piece to F in this way, lastly prepare the narrow and long edge of piece 3 over G to H; then prepare the shoulder and neckline edges from H to I.

Joining the Back Piece

Join the second piece 2 with the first on a narrow edge from I to B; prepare the long edge of piece 2 to J. Join piece 8 with piece 2; prepare the narrow edge of piece 8. Join piece 6 first with piece 8; then with piece 2, prepare the narrow edge of piece 6. Join piece 7 with the pieces 6 and 2 and on the shoulder edge with

		Holes			Cast on			Number of rows			Color	Application
Piece	Number	36/38	40/42	44/46	36/38	40/42	44/46	36/38	40/42	44/46		
1	6	3 x 39	3 x 39	3 x 39	9	9	9	154	154	154	Natural	F / B
2	2	3 x 39	5 x 39	7 x 39	9	15	21	154	154	154	Natural	F / B
3	2	39 x 3	39 x 5	39 x 7	117	117	117	10	18	26	Brown	F / B
4	2	3 x 31	3 x 31	3 x 31	9	9	9	122	122	122	Brown	F / B
5	2	23 x 3	23 x 3	23 x 3	69	69	69	10	10	10	Brown	F / B
6	2	3 x 15	3 x 15	3 x 15	9	9	9	58	58	58	Natural	F / B
7	2	3 x 15	3 x 15	3 x 15	9	9	9	58	58	58	Brown	F / B
8	2	3 x 7	3 x 7	3 x 7	9	9	9	26	26	26	Brown	F / B
9	2	3 x 7	3 x 7	3 x 7	9	9	9	26	26	26	Natural	F / B
10	2	3 x 15	3 x 15	3 x 15	9	9	9	58	58	58	Natural	F / B
11	4	23 x 13 x 15	23 x 13 x 15	23 x 13 x 15	69	69	69	50	50	50	Brown	Sleeve

F = Front piece, B = back piece

the first piece 7, the first shoulder seam is closed. Then prepare the free long edges of pieces 7, 6, and 8 from E to K. Attach all remaining strips for the back piece in this way, however, for the neckline (red line), do not join the following strips 1, 5, 1, and 4 with the strips of the front piece – instead, only prepare the narrow edges. For the second shoulder seam join the following strips 1 and 3 as before on the shoulder edge with the strips of the front piece, end at H. Cut off the yarn.

Attaching the Sleeves

Attach the yarn at point I on the front sleeve: Join sleeve piece 11 with piece 2 from I to M. Prepare piece 11 from M over N and O to I. Join the second piece 11 with the first from I to O (= top sleeve seam); prepare the free edge of the second sleeve piece from O to N and join the sleeve pieces from N to M (= bottom sleeve seam). Prepare piece 11 from M to I; work the junction to the first piece 11 and to the second piece 2 on the back piece. Join pieces 11 and 2 from I to M; then join the pieces 2 of the back and front side from M to A (= 1st side seam). For the edge finish, prepare the bottom back piece edge from A to G. Cut off the yarn.

Newly attach the yarn at H on the front sleeve: Attach the 2nd sleeve inversely, close the 2nd side seam to G.

3. Finishing

Continue crocheting as follows for the hem from G in natural: **1st round** – Proceed with 3 slip stitches to the following chain stitch between two clusters; 3 chain stitches count as the 1st double crochet stitch and 1 double crochet stitch around the chain stitch (with 1 chain stitch, skip 3 stitches of the edge finish, 2 double crochet stitches around the following chain stitch). Always repeat; end with 1 chain stitch and 1 slip stitch in the 3rd beginning chain stitch. **2nd round** – Proceed with 2 slip stitches to the following chain stitch (2 single crochet stitches around the chain stitch; with 1 chain stitch, skip 2 stitches of the preceding round). Always repeat; end with 1 slip stitch in the 1st single crochet stitch. **3rd round** – Crochet reverse single crochets (= single crochet stitches from left to right). Likewise, crochet around the sleeve edges. Newly attach the yarn at E in natural and crochet around the neckline with 1 round of reverse single crochets.

Knitting Chart
Piece 11

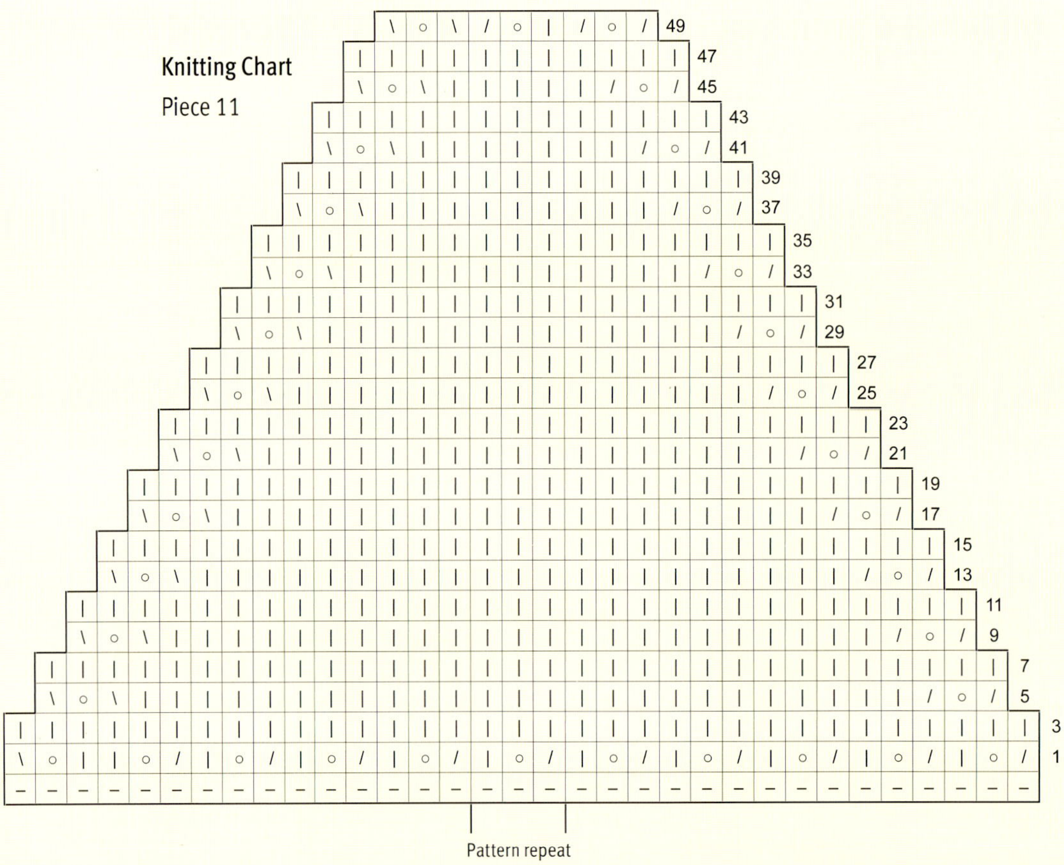

Diagram

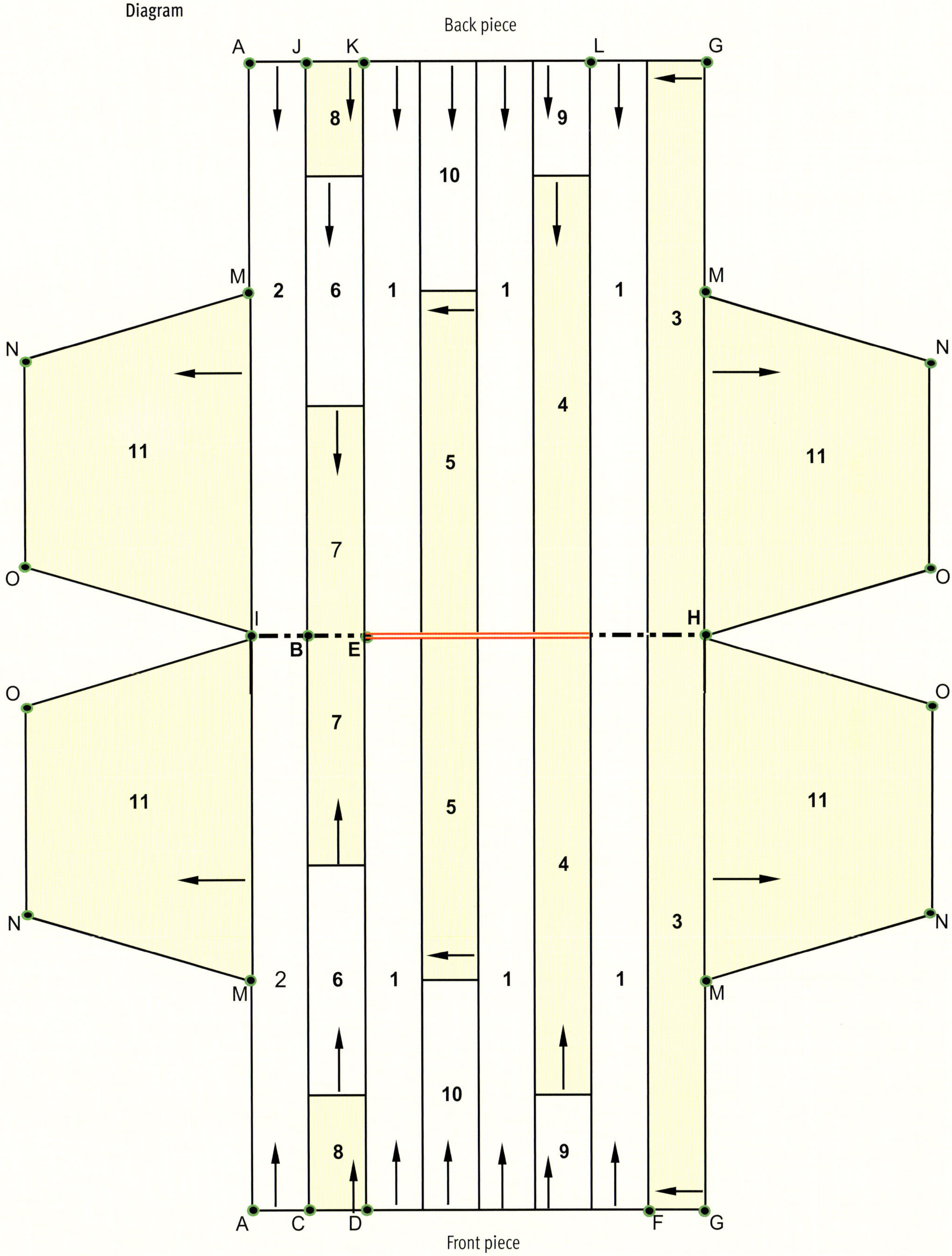
Back piece
A
J
K
L
G
8
9
10
M
2
6
1
1
1
M
3
N
N
4
5
11
11
7
O
O
I
H
B
E
O
O
7
11
11
5
4
N
N
3
M
2
6
1
1
1
M
10
8
9
A
C
D
F
G
Front piece

Simply Slip In!

Goodbye Cold Feet

Level of difficulty: Intermediate
Size: Sm: 37-39 {M: 40-42; Lg: 43-45}, equivalent to U.S. shoe sizes 6-8, 8-9, & 10-13
Material: Decorative sock yarn (55% polyamide, 45% virgin wool), or substitute any worsted yarn that knits to gauge; 1¾ oz (50g)/ 130m (143 yds per skein). Berry: Sm: 2 skeins [3½ oz (100g), 282 yds] {M: 3 skeins [5¼ oz (150g), 429 yds]; Lg: 4 skeins 7 oz (200g), 572 yds]}.
Knitting needles: US 6 (4.25mm)
Crochet hook: US H/7 (4.25mm)
Basic pattern: Stockinette stitch
Stitch gauge: 20 stitches and 32 rows = 4" x 4" (10 cm x 10 cm)

1. Knitting the Individual Pieces

According to table, knit 3 different individual pieces at the specified quantity = 8 pieces total. The number of stitches and rows, as well as the application, are specified. Knit according to the general knitting chart for squares and rectangles (see page 6), except for heel piece 3. Work this according to the knitting chart, at the same time working the pattern repeat 7/9/11 times.

2. Joining the Individual Pieces

Two pieces are always joined by preparation and closing (see pages 8 - 9), even if this is not always explicitly mentioned in the text.

Sole and toe

As described in the slippers course on pages 10 to 13, join piece 1 with piece 2, in the process carrying out the work steps 1 to 5 according to the appropriate diagram.

Heel (Diagram below)

Double each 2 heel pieces, each with the wrong sides together and work together = doubled piece 3. On the folded in edges of piece 1 cast on the yarn for size 37-39 between the 2nd and 3rd hole, for size 40-42 between the 3rd and 4th hole, and for size 43-45 between the 4th and 5th hole at A on a chain stitch between 2 clusters. Join the doubled piece 3 on the diagonal edge over 3 holes with piece 1 (blue arrows); then work two clusters in the corner hole of piece 3, however, join this with 2 holes of piece 1 (red arrows). Then join the bottom edge of piece 3 with piece 1 (blue arrows), at the same time working two clusters in the second corner hole again and joining with two holes of piece 1 (red arrows). Lastly, join the second diagonal edge of doubled piece 3 with the remaining holes of piece 1 to B. Subsequently, combine the two layers of the top edge of doubled piece 2 by preparation.

3. Finishing

Crochet around the border of the opening with a round of reverse single crochets (= single crochet stitches from left to right).

Knitting chart
Piece 3

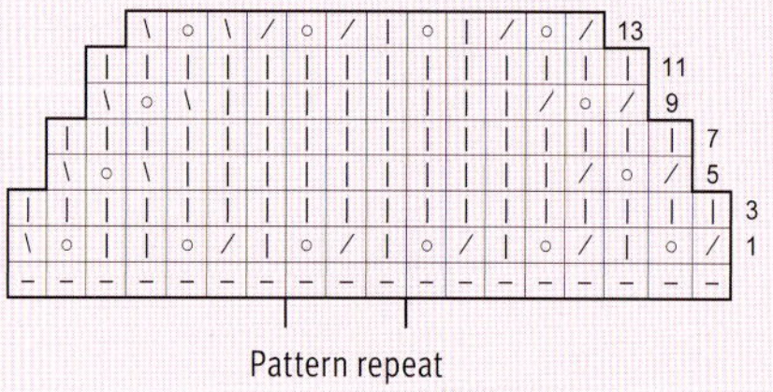

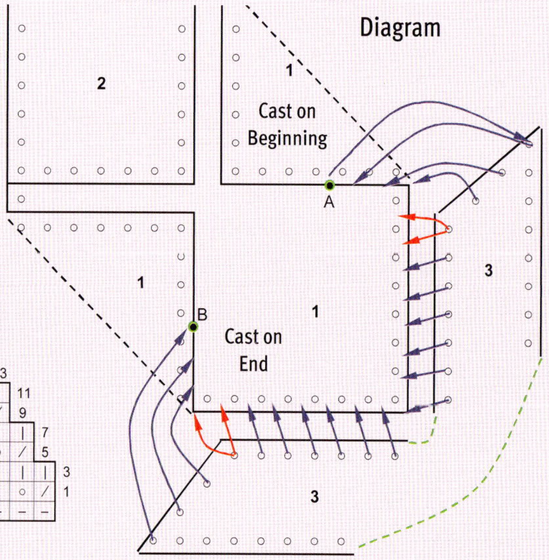

		Holes			Cast on			Number of rows			Application
Piece	Number	37 - 39	40 - 42	43 - 45	37 - 39	40 - 42	43 - 45	37 - 39	40 - 42	43 - 45	
1	2	11 x 11	13 x 13	15 x 15	33	39	45	42	50	58	Sole/side piece
2	2	5 x 5	6 x 6	7 x 7	15	18	21	18	22	26	Toe
3	4	12 x 4 x 10	14 x 4 x 12	16 x 4 x 14	36	42	48	14	14	14	Heel piece

Everyone Wants Them

Slippers with Pompom Trim

Level of difficulty: Intermediate

Material: Sports weight wool (100% virgin wool), or substitute any sport weight yarn that knits to gauge; 1$^3/_4$ oz (50g)/125m (137 yds per skein). Chili, rust, and cognac or green tones: 1 skein each [1$^3/_4$ oz (50g), 137 yds, each].

Pompom yarn (100% polyester), 1$^3/_4$ oz (50g)/80m (88 yds per skein). Rust or green: 4 skeins [7 oz (200g), 352 yds]. 2 toggle closures.

Knitting needles: US 6 (4.25mm)

Crochet hook: US H/7 (4.25mm)

Note: Knit the individual pieces from virgin wool, and also work the crochet junctions in virgin wool. Only use the pompom yarn for the edge finish.

Basic pattern: Stockinette stitch

Stitch gauge: 22 stitches and 32 rows = 4" x 4" (10 cm x 10 cm)

1. Knitting the Individual Pieces

According to the table, knit 5 different individual pieces at the specified quantity = 10 pieces total. The number of stitches and rows, as well as the color and application, are specified. Knit according to the general knitting chart for squares and rectangles (see page 6).

Arrange the individual pieces according to the diagrams 1 and 2 on pages 10 and 13. The diagrams show the individual pieces of the 3rd size, work similarly for the 1st and 2nd size, however, with a correspondingly smaller number of holes.

2. Joining the Individual Pieces

Join the individual pieces in chili according to the diagrams, photographs, and working steps 1 to 13 in the course on pages 10 to 13; the variant colors in the photographs serve only to clarify the steps. Two pieces are always joined by preparation and closing (see pages 8 - 9), even if this is not always explicitly mentioned in the text.

3. Finishing

The reverse stockinette of the slipper first remains outside.

Then continue working with pompom yarn for the edge finish, thereby always working only the thin sections of the yarn; place the bobbles in between behind the work and do not pull through, so later they will be located on the outside of the slipper. For the 1st row, insert into the 1st single crochet stitch; draw 1 loop from a thin yarn location and work 1 chain stitch. (Place the following bobble backward and work 2 chain stitches with the following thin yarn location; place the following bobble backward, skip a cluster, and work 1 single crochet stitch with thin yarn around the chain stitch after the cluster) Always repeat; end with 1 single crochet stitch at the end of the 1st row.

Tip: A bobble is always carried along at the back and the second only cast on. This results in a larger space and the work does not pucker.

Pull the finished slipper over a sleeve ironing board and carefully steam the toe, heel, and side parts with the steam iron. On each slipper, pull a toggle closure through the center holes of the side piece edges and turn.

		Holes			Cast on			Number or rows			Application	Color
Piece	Number	36 - 39	40 - 42	43 - 45	36 - 39	40 - 42	43 - 45	36 - 39	40 - 42	43 - 45		
1	2	11 x 11	13 x 13	15 x 15	33	39	45	42	50	58	Sole	Chili
2	2	5 x 5	6 x 6	7 x 7	15	18	21	18	22	26	Toe	Cognac
3	2	5 x 5	6 x 6	7 x 7	15	18	21	18	22	26	Heel	Cognac
4	2	5 x 5	6 x 6	7 x 7	15	18	21	18	22	26	Side	Rust
5	2	5 x 5	6 x 6	7 x 7	15	18	21	18	22	26	Side	Rust

Something Fits In!

Handbag with Floral Granny Squares

Level of difficulty: Experienced

Size: $17^3/_4$" x $19^5/_8$" (45 cm x 50 cm) (without handle)

Material: Ribbon yarn (51% cotton, 49% polyacrylic), or substitute any heavy worsted yarn that knits to gauge; $1^3/_4$ oz (50g)/75m (82 yds per skein). Sky blue: 7 skeins [$12^1/_4$ oz (350g), 574 yds]. Aqua: 4 skeins [7 oz (200g), 328 yds]. 2 toggle closures.

Knitting needles: US 6 (4mm)

Crochet hook: US G/6 (4.5mm)

Basic pattern: Stockinette stitch

Granny square: Description and crochet diagram as with model "shrug" on page 30.

Stitch gauge: Basic pattern 16 stitches and 24 rows = 4" x 4" (10 cm x 10 cm); granny square = approximately $3^1/_2$" x $3^1/_2$" (9 cm x 9 cm)

1. Knitting/Crocheting the Individual Pieces

According to the table, knit 6 different individual pieces at the specified quantity = 18 pieces total. The number of stitches and rows, as well as the color and application are specified. Knit according to the general knitting chart for squares and rectangles (see page 6). Additionally, knit 6 granny squares.

Arrange the individual pieces according to the diagrams on this page and on pages 62 and 63; arrows on the diagrams = working direction of the individual pieces.

2. Joining the Individual Pieces

Crochet together the individual pieces according to the general crochet diagram (see page 8) and the diagrams 1 to 4 in aqua. The granny squares are each worked with a piece 4. Two pieces are always joined by preparation and closing (see pages 8 - 9), even if this is not always explicitly mentioned in the text.

Working the Patch Piece (Diagram 1)

For the patch piece, arrange the pieces 3 and 4 with the wrong sides together on a piece 1 (inside piece) according to diagram 1. Place a granny square with the wrong and right sides together on the outer pieces 4, the center piece 4 (red) remains free.

Diagram 1

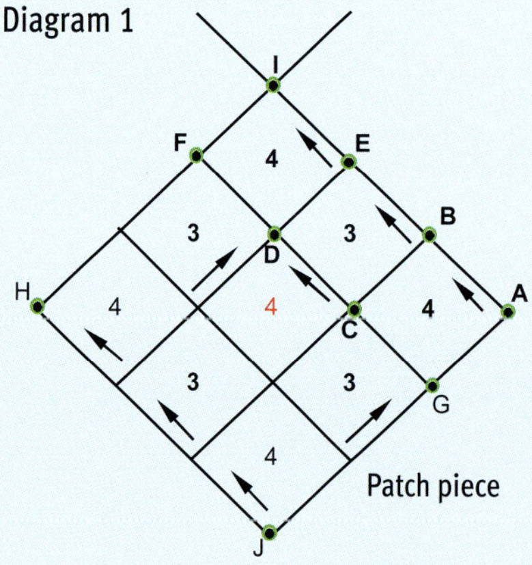

Patch piece

Begin at A. Combine piece 1 with piece 4 + granny square from A to B by preparation, including the granny square only at the locations on the crochet diagram marked with arrows A, C, and E. In the same way, combine the edges of piece 4 and granny square from B to C by preparation. Join piece 3 with piece 4 from C to B; then combine piece 3 and piece 1 from B to E by preparation. Prepare the third edge of piece 3 from E to D alone. Join piece 4 + granny square with piece 3, then combine the edges of pieces 1 and 4 + granny square from E over I to F by preparation; subsequently, prepare all edges from F over D and C to G. In the same way, attach the 2nd strip with the pieces 3, 4, and 3 on the first and the 3rd strip with the pieces 4 + granny square and 3 and 4 + granny square on the 2nd strip; then combine the edge to H by preparation. Then combine the outer edges of all pieces that are not yet crocheted with piece 1 from H over J, G to A by preparation. Do not cut off the yarn.

Piece	Number	Holes	Cast on	Number of rows	Color	Application
1	3	17 x 17	51	66	Sky blue	2 x outside / 1 x inside
2	2	17 x 17	51	66	Aqua	Inside
3	4	5 x 5	15	18	Sky blue	Patch, outside
4	7	5 x 5	15	18	Aqua	Patch, outside
5	1	3 x 30	9	118	Sky blue	Handle outside
6	1	3 x 30	9	118	Aqua	Handle inside

Joining the Patch Piece with the Side Pieces (Diagram 2)

For each side piece, place a piece 1 and a piece 2 with the wrong sides together on top of each other and work together = doubled piece. The diagram 2 shows the front side of the pocket, letters for the back side are in parentheses. Begin at A on the patch piece: Join the patch piece with the doubled piece 1 + 2 from A to I on the front side and from I to H on the back side. Then combine the edges of the doubled piece from H over K back to the front side to A by preparation. Likewise, join the second doubled piece with the patch piece from A over J to H; then combine the edges from H over L to A by preparation. Cut off the yarn.

Pocket Opening (Diagram 3)

For the front side, place a granny square with the wrong and right sides together on a piece 4, fold both pieces diagonally, and work together as follows. Join piece 4 + granny square on 2 edges (these lie fourfold) with the doubled pieces 1 + 2 from M over A to N (see diagram 2). For a better overview, on diagram 3 only the crochet edge on piece 4 is illustrated with the arrows for the connecting single crochet stitches; the already existing crochet edge on the doubled pieces is not shown. Likewise, attach the last piece 4 + granny square from P over H to O on the backside.

Attaching the Handle (Diagram 4)

Place pieces 5 and 6 on top of each other with the wrong sides together and combine a long edge by preparation. Join the first narrow edge

Diagram 2

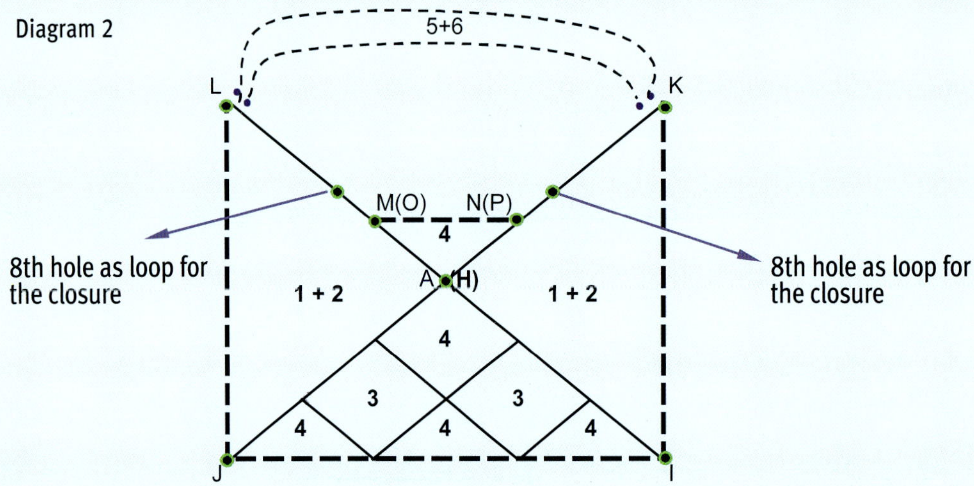

Diagram 3

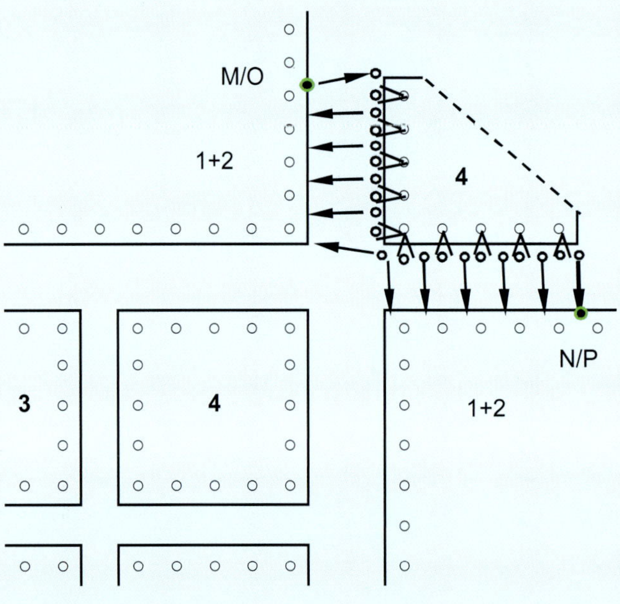

with the corner of the doubled piece (see L on diagram 2) according to diagram 4 by preparation and closing, working two clusters in the center hole of the handle narrow side as shown in red.

Tip: For a better overview, only the crochet edge on piece 5 + 6 is illustrated with the blue arrows for the connecting single crochet stitches; the already existing crochet edge on the doubled pieces 1 + 2 is not illustrated. Combine the second long edge by preparation and also join the second narrow edge with the corner of the second side piece (see K on diagram 2). Cut off the yarn.

Diagram 4

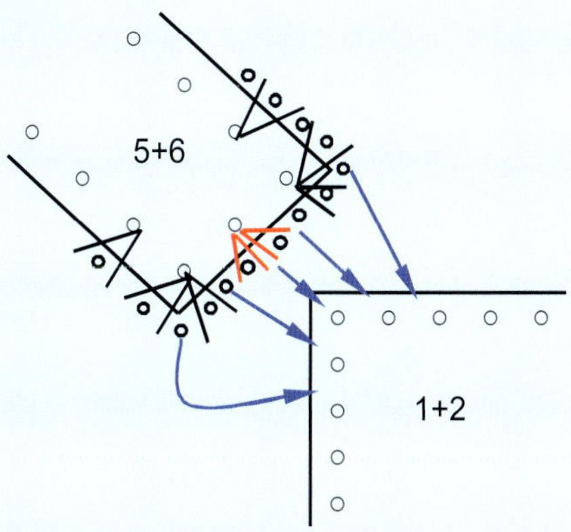

3. Finishing

For the edge finish, newly attach at M on the front side according to diagram 2 in sky blue. Crochet over the prepared edge from M to L, the handle edge to K, and the second edge to N once again with clusters as follows: Work 1 single crochet stitch + 1 chain stitch + 1 single crochet stitch between 2 clusters of the aqua-colored edge, with 1 chain stitch skip 3 stitches of the aqua-colored edge. Always repeat. Lastly, work a row of reverse single crochets (= single crochet stitches from left to right) in sky blue. Likewise, crochet over the pocket back side and second handle edge from P to O.

On the front and back side over the 8th hole crochet on 1 loop each in sky blue. For this, attach on the border, crochet an approximately 2 3/8" (6 cm) length of chain stitches, cast on, turn with 1 chain stitch, crochet over the loop tightly with single crochet stitches, and cast on again. Put the closures through the loops and turn.

Beginner Easy

Pillow with Turn Effect

Level of difficulty: Beginner

Size: Pillow 1 and 2: 19⅝" x 19⅝" (50 cm x 50 cm); Pillow 3: 13¾" x 13¾" (35 cm x 35 cm)

Material: Bouclé sock yarn (65% polyamide, 35% superwash virgin wool), or substitute any heavy sport weight yarn that knits to gauge; 1¾ oz (50g)/125m (137 yds per skein). **Pillow 1:** black and off-white: 3 skeins each [5¼ oz (150g), 411 yds, each]. Emerald and purple: 1 skein each [1¾ oz (50g), 137 yds, each]. 4 white buttons. **Pillow 2:** black and off-white: 3 skeins each [5¼ oz (150g), 411 yds, each]. Emerald and purple: 1 skein each [1¾ oz (50g), 137 yds, each]. 5 white buttons. **Pillow 3:** emerald: 2 skeins [3½ oz (100g), 274 yds]. Black: 1 skein, [1¾ oz (50g), 137 yds]. 4 black buttons.

Knitting needles: US 4 (3.5mm)

Crochet hook: US D/3 (3 to 3.25mm)

Basic pattern: Stockinette stitch

Stitch gauge: 22 stitches and 26 rows = 4" x 4" (10 cm x 10 cm)

Pillow 1

1. Knitting the Individual Pieces

According to the table, knit 5 different individual pieces at the specified quantity = 12 pieces total. The number of stitches and rows, as well as the color and application, are specified. Knit according to the general knitting chart for squares and rectangles (see page 6).

Arrange the individual pieces according to diagram 1 on page 66; arrows on the diagram = working direction of the individual pieces. Arrange the pieces marked with the addition "Li" on the diagram with the wrong side = reverse stockinette outward, arrange all remaining pieces with the right = stockinette outward.

2. Joining the Individual Pieces

Crochet together the individual pieces, according to the general crochet diagram (see page 8) and diagram 1, with black on the front and off-white on the back The same points on the diagram meet. Two pieces are always joined by preparation and closing (see pages 8 - 9), even if this is not always explicitly mentioned in the text.

Front

Begin at point A piece 1: Prepare three sides of piece 1 over B and C to D. Join the first piece 1 with the second to C; prepare two edges over E to F. Join piece 2 with the second piece 1 to E, prepare two edges over G to I. Join piece 5 with piece 2 to J; prepare the long edge to K. Join piece 3 with piece 5 to J and with piece 2 to H; prepare the third edge to L. Join piece 4 with piece 3 to H and with piece 2 to G; then prepare the remaining outer edges to A.

Back

Begin at point A piece 1: Work the back inversely, thereby for the opening joining both pieces 1 first over 15 holes; then for the opening only , prepare 14 holes. Join the remaining 2 holes again. After joining all pieces, prepare all remaining outer edges to A.

Pillow 1

Piece	Number	Holes	Cast on	Number of rows	Color	Application
1	2	3 x 31	9	122	White	F
1	2	3 x 31	9	122	Black	B
2	1	7 x 31	21	122	White	F
2	1	7 x 31	21	122	Black	B
3	1	15 x 19	45	74	White	F
3	1	15 x 19	45	74	Black	B
4	1	3 x 15	9	58	White	F
4	1	3 x 15	9	58	Black	B
5	2	7 x 15	21	58	Emerald	F + B

F = front side, B = back side

3. Finishing

Crochet on four button loops from chain stitches at the size of the buttons evenly distributed on the second piece 1 of the back on the opening in off-white and crochet over the loops, each decreasing tightly with single crochet stitches. Sew on the buttons correspondingly on the first piece 1.

Place the front and back with the insides facing each other and crochet together in black as follows: **1st round** – Attach on a corner between two clusters of the edging, work 1 chain stitch and 1 single crochet stitch around both corner chain stitches of the right and wrong sides (skip the following cluster with 1 chain stitch, work 2 single crochet stitches around the chain stitches of the right and wrong sides). Always repeat, end with 1 chain stitch and 1 slip stitch in the beginning chain stitch. **2nd round** – Proceed with 2 slip stitches to the chain stitch between 2 clusters, work 1 chain stitch and 1 single crochet stitch around the chain stitch of the preceding round (with 1 chain stitch, skip the cluster of the preceding round; work 2 single crochet stitches around the chain stitch.) Always repeat; end with 1 chain stitch and 1 slip stitch in the beginning chain stitch. **3rd round** – like the 2nd round. **4th round** – Crochet reverse single crochets (= single crochet stitches from left to right).

Pillow 2

1. Knitting the Individual Pieces

Like pillow 1; however, according to the table on the following page, knit 7 different individual pieces at the specified quantity = 14 pieces total.

2. Joining the Individual Pieces

Crochet together the individual pieces according to the general crochet diagram (see page 8) and diagram 2, with black on the front and off-white on the back. The same points on the diagram meet. Two pieces are always joined by preparation and closing (see pages 8 - 9), even if this is not explicitly mentioned.

Front

Begin at point A piece 1: Prepare piece 1 over B, C, and D to A all around. Join piece 2 with piece 1 to D, prepare two edges of piece 2 over G to I. Join piece 3 with piece 2 to H, prepare an edge to J. Join piece 4 with piece 3 to H and with piece 2 to G, prepare a narrow edge to K. Join piece 7 with piece 4 to G, prepare an edge to N. Join piece 6 with piece 7 to G and with piece 2 to D, prepare a narrow edge to F. Join piece 5 with piece 6 to D and with piece 1 to C, prepare the remaining outer edges to A.

Diagram 1

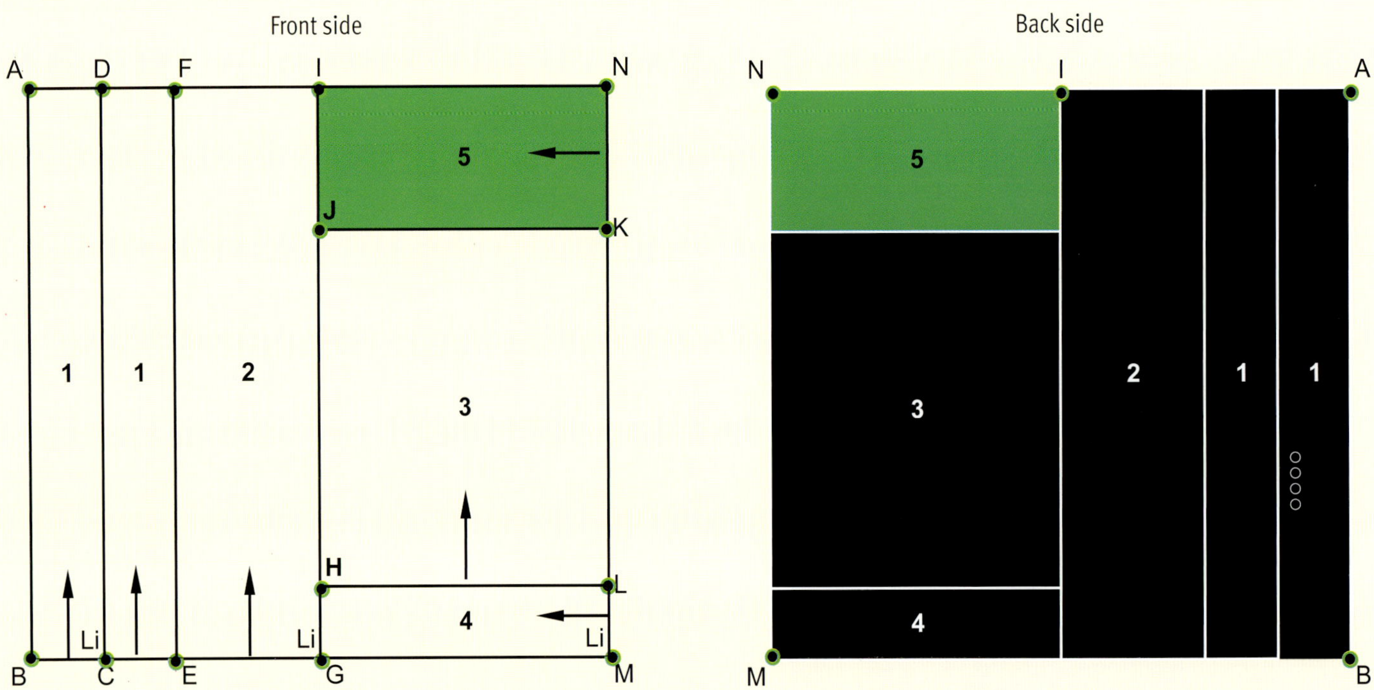

Back

Begin at point A piece 1 and prepare piece 1 all around. Then work the back inversely, joining piece 2 first over 3 holes with piece 1; then only prepare 18 holes of piece 2 for the opening. Join the remaining 6 holes with piece 1 again. After joining all pieces, prepare the remaining outer edges to A.

3. Finishing

At piece 2 on the opening, crochet on five evenly distributed button loops from chain stitches in off-white at the size of the buttons and crochet over the loops, decreasing tightly with single crochet stitches. Sew the buttons correspondingly on piece 1. Crochet together the front and back as with pillow 1.

Pillow 2

Piece	Number	Holes	Cast on	Number of rows	Color	Application
1	1	7 x 27	21	106	White	F
1	1	7 x 27	21	106	Black	B
2	1	19 x 27	57	106	White	F
2	1	19 x 27	57	106	Black	B
3	2	3 x 3	9	10	Purple	F + B
4	1	3 x 23	9	90	White	F
4	1	3 x 23	9	90	Black	B
5	2	3 x 7	9	26	Emerald	F + B
6	1	3 x 19	9	74	White	F
6	1	3 x 19	9	74	Black	B
7	1	3 x 19	9	74	White	F
7	1	3 x 3	9	10	Black	B

F= front side, B = back side

Diagram 2

Front side

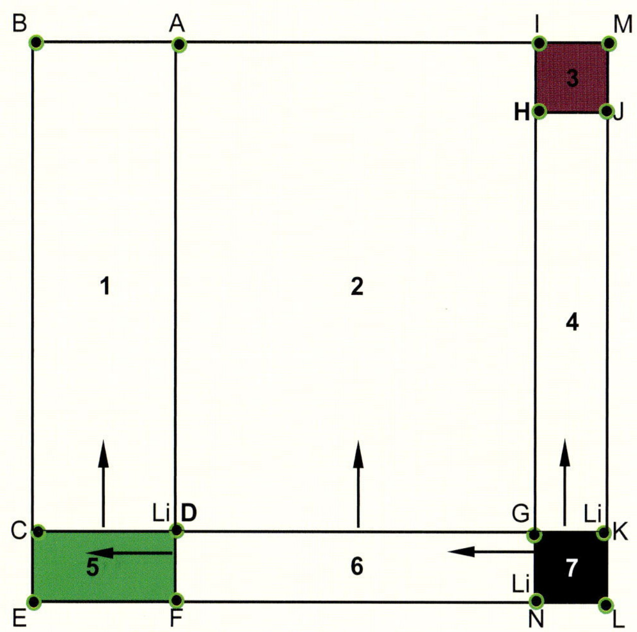

Back side

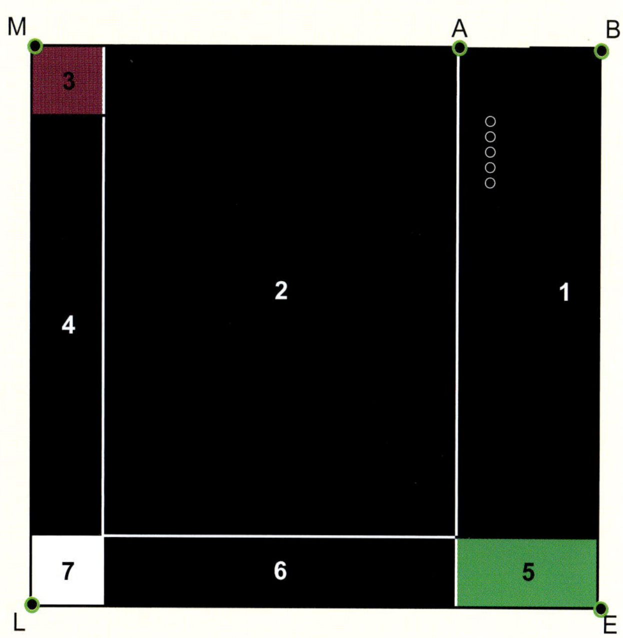

Pillow 3

1. Knitting the Individual Pieces

Like pillow 1; however, according to the table below, knit 3 different individual pieces.

2. Joining the Individual Pieces

Crochet together the individual pieces according to the general crochet diagram (see page 8) and diagram 3 with black on the front and off-white on the back. The same points on the diagram meet. Two pieces are always joined by preparation and closing (see pages 8 - 9), even if this is not always explicitly mentioned.

Front

Begin at A piece 1: Prepare piece 1 over B, C and D to A all around. Cut off the yarn. At B, newly attach piece 2. Prepare piece 2 on three edges over F and E to C, join the fourth edge from C over 3 holes with piece 1; then for the opening only prepare 14 holes. Join the remaining 3 holes of piece 2 with piece 1 to B again.

Back

Begin at D piece 3 and prepare piece 3 all around.

3. Finishing

On piece 1 on the opening, crochet on four evenly distributed button loops from chain stitches in black at the size of the buttons and crochet over the loops, each decreasing tightly with single crochet stitches. Sew the buttons on piece 2 correspondingly. Crochet together the front and back side as with pillow 1.

Pillow 3

Piece	Number	Holes	Cast on	Number of rows	Color	Application
1	1	5 x 20	15	78	Emerald	F
2	1	14 x 20	42	78	Emerald	F
3	1	20 x 20	60	78	Emerald	B

F = Front side, B = back side

Diagram 3

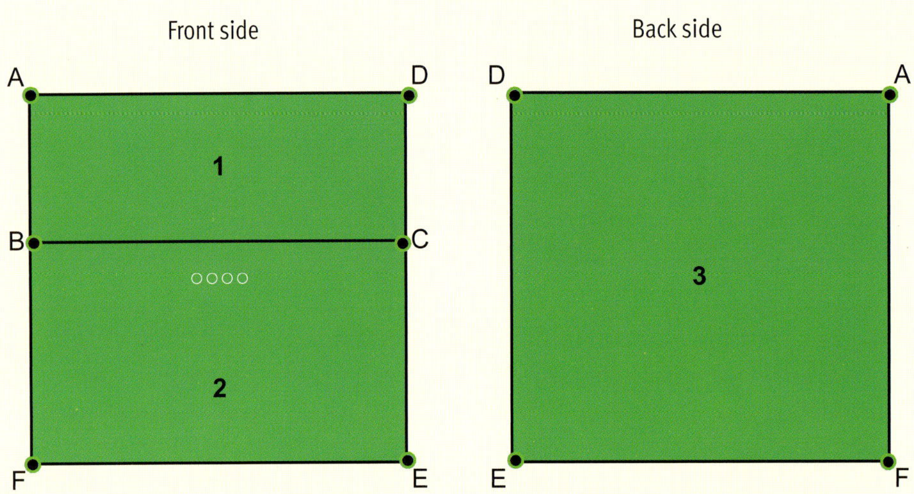

Warm & Decorative

Reversible Throw

Level of difficulty: Intermediate

Size: Approximately 43 1/4" x 62" (110 cm x 160 cm)

Material: Bouclé yarn (75% mohair, 17% virgin wool, 9% polyacrylic), or substitute any chunky weight yarn that knits to gauge; 1 3/4 oz (50g)/50m (55 yds per skein). Ochre, red, reddish brown, and brown: 5 skeins each [8¾ oz (250g), 275 yds, each].

Thicker wool yarn (51% virgin wool, 49% polyacrylic); 1 3/4 oz (50g)/85m (93 yds per skein). Natural: 15 skeins [26¼ oz (750g), 1395 yds].

Knitting needles: US 10 (6mm)

Crochet hook: US J/10 (6mm)

Basic pattern: Stockinette stitch

Stitch gauge: Bouclé yarn 12 stitches and 18 rows = 4" x 4" (10 cm x 10 cm); wool yarn 13 stitches and 20 rows = 4" x 4" (10 cm x 10 cm)

1. Knitting the Individual Pieces

According to the table, knit 6 different individual pieces at the specified quantity = 118 pieces total. Knit the pieces 1, 2, 3, and 4 for the front and back side in different colors. The number of stitches and rows, as well as color and application, are specified. Knit according to the general knitting chart for squares and rectangles (see page 6).

Arrange the individual pieces according to the diagram on page 73. Arrange the pieces marked with the addition "Re" on the diagram with the front side = stockinette outward, arrange all remaining pieces with the back side = reverse stockinette outward. Arrows on the diagram = working direction of the individual pieces.

2. Joining the Individual Pieces

Crochet together the individual pieces according to the general crochet diagram (see page 8) and the diagram in natural.

Two pieces are always joined by preparation and closing (see pages 8 - 9), even if this is not always explicitly mentioned in the text.

Place the reddish brown pieces 1 of the front side with the right sides together on the brown pieces 1 of the back side and always work together as doubled piece 1. Proceed with pieces 2 likewise = doubled piece 2.

Place the red pieces 3 of the front side with the right sides together on the ocher-colored pieces 3 of the back side and always work together as doubled pieces 3. Proceed with pieces 4 likewise = doubled piece 4. During the preparation of the doubled pieces, both layers are combined. During preparation and closing of doubled pieces, both layers are combined and joined as one piece with the adjoining piece at the same time.

1st Side Piece

Begin at A piece 2 for the first block: Prepare doubled piece 2 on two edges over B to C. Join piece 5 with piece 2 to D by preparation and closing; prepare an edge to E. Join doubled piece 1 first with piece 5 from E to D, then with doubled piece 2 from D to B. Then prepare the edges of the pieces 1, 5, and 2 over F, E, G and C to H.

Join the following doubled piece 1 with doubled piece 2 from H to C; prepare the long edge to I. Join the second piece 5 with doubled piece 1 from I to C and with the first piece 5 from C to G, prepare the edges over J and I to K. Join the second doubled piece 2 with the pieces 1 and 5 from K to J; prepare two edges over L to M. The first block of 6 pieces is finished. Attach the individual pieces of the following 2 blocks according to the diagram step by step correspondingly, end at point N.

Piece	Number	Holes	Cast on	Number of rows	Color	Application
1	18	3 x 7	9	26	Reddish brown	Front side
1	18	3 x 7	9	26	Brown	Back side
2	8	3 x 11	9	42	Reddish brown	Front side
2	8	3 x 11	9	42	Brown	Back side
3	12	3 x 7	9	26	Red	Front side
3	12	3 x 7	9	26	Ochre	Back side
4	12	3 x 11	9	42	Red	Front side
4	12	3 x 11	9	42	Ochre	Back side
5	16	7 x 7	21	26	Natural	FS + BS
6	2	15 x 15	45	58	Natural	FS + BS

Center Piece

At N, skip to doubled piece 3 and join this with piece 1 from N to A; prepare the long edge of doubled piece 3 to B. Join piece 5 first with doubled piece 3 from B to A; then join with the preceding piece 5 from A to C. Prepare edges over D and B to E. Join doubled piece 4 with the pieces 3 and 5 from E over B to D; prepare two edges over G to F. Join the second doubled piece 4 with the first from F to G; prepare edges over H and K to I. Join doubled piece 3 from I to K with piece 4; prepare the long edge to J. Join piece 5 first from J to K with doubled piece 3, then from K to H with doubled piece 4; prepare edge to L.

Join the third doubled piece 4 from L to M with piece 5; prepare two edges to N. Join the doubled pieces 1 and 4; prepare long edge to O. Join piece 6 from O to Q with the pieces 1 and 4, then to P. Join the first doubled piece 1 with piece 6; prepare the narrow edge to G. Join both doubled pieces 1 on the narrow edges; join the second doubled piece 1 with piece 6 to Q and with piece 4 to M, then join the long edges of both doubled pieces 1 with the pieces 5, 4, 4, and 5 to R. Prepare pieces 1 and 6 from R over P to S. Join doubled piece 1 with piece 6; prepare the narrow edge. Join doubled piece 4 with doubled piece 1, then with pieces 6 and 1 to R, then with piece 5 to C, and lastly, with all adjoining pieces of the 1st side piece to T. Prepare the bottom edge from T over S and O to U.

For the center border at U junction to the doubled piece 3 and join this with doubled piece 1 to O; prepare the long edge 3. Join the doubled pieces 1 and 3 to O, then join doubled piece 1 with piece 6, and prepare the second long edge. Also attach the doubled pieces 3, 3, 1 and 3, joining the last doubled piece 3 also with the adjoining pieces 5 of the 1st side piece to V; then prepare the complete bottom edge of the center border to X. Junction to doubled piece 1 and join this with piece 3; prepare the long and narrow edges. Join doubled piece 4 with piece 1, prepare the long edge. Join the following doubled piece 1 with piece 4; prepare the long and narrow edge. Join both doubled pieces 1, prepare the long edge. Join piece 6 with the pieces 1, 1, 4, 1, and the border pieces to W; then prepare the last edge of piece 6 and narrow edge of piece 1 to Y. Join doubled piece 4 with piece 1 and 6; prepare the narrow edge to L. Join the doubled piece 1 first with piece 4 then with piece 6 to W and with piece 3 to V; then join the edges of the pieces 1 and 4 with the 1st side piece to G. Lastly, prepare the bottom edges of the pieces 4, 1, 1, and 4.

Join piece 5 with the doubled pieces 4 and 1; then prepare 2 edges. Join the doubled piece 3 with piece 5, prepare the narrow edge. Join doubled piece 4 with the pieces 3 and 5; then join with piece 1. Prepare the long edge. Join both doubled pieces 4; then join the second piece 4 with piece 1. Prepare the long edge. Join the doubled piece 3 with piece 4; prepare the long edge to E. Join piece 5 first with piece 3 then with piece 4 and on the third edge with the pieces 1 and 4 to G. Join piece 5 and piece 3 on the least edge with the 1st side piece; end at F. Cut off the yarn.

2nd Side Piece

Work the 2nd side piece like the 1st; end at N. Then turn the second side piece 180 degrees so that it lies inversely to the first, and place on the center piece according to the diagram. Place the center piece on the 2nd side piece with the right sides together and join the inner edges of both pieces from N by preparation and closing.

3. Finishing

Prepare the remaining outer edges in natural, then crochet around the outer edges with a round of reverse bobble stitches (see page 20) in natural.

Diagram

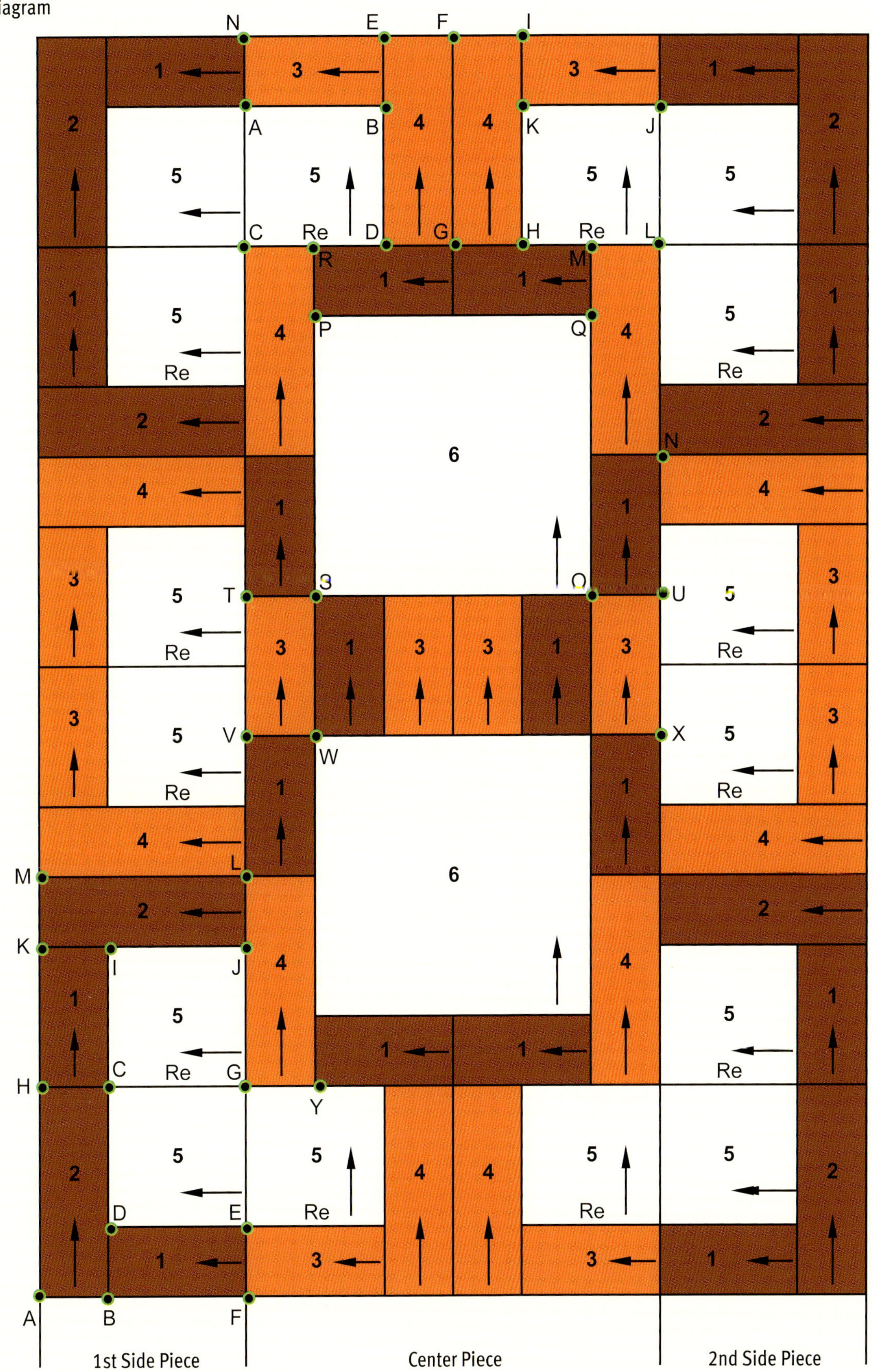

Basic Course in Knitting

Cast On

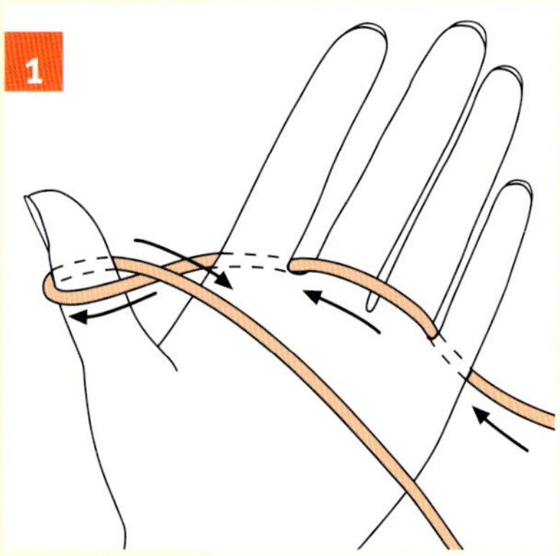

Place the end yarn between the little finger and ring finger from the outside in, between the middle and index finger outward, and from the front around the thumb.

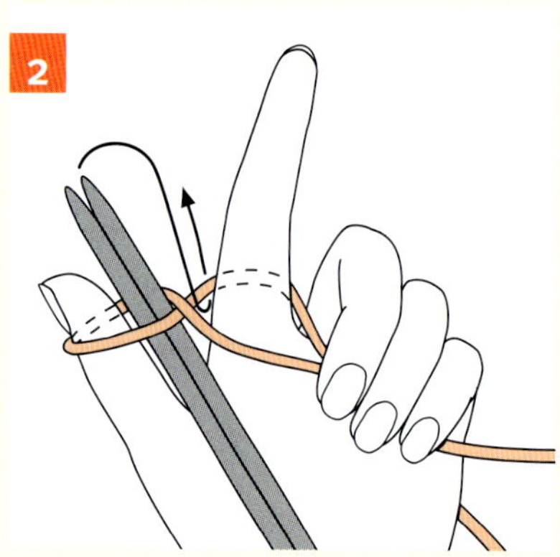

With 2 needles, catch the thumb loop. Then with the needles, catch the index finger loop of the yarn. Draw the index finger loop through the thumb loop.

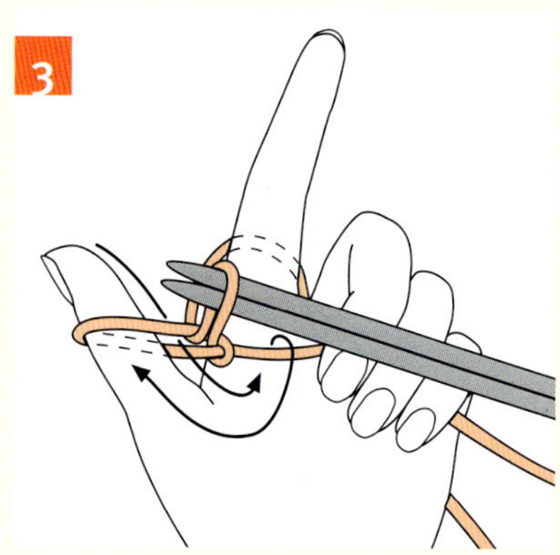

Pull the thumb from the loop, lead under the front yarn and pull the loop tight with the thumb. Always repeat steps 2 and 3. Withdraw the 2nd needle after the desired number of stitches.

Knit Stitches

Take the needle with the stitches into the left hand. The yarn lies behind the left needle. With the right needle, insert into the stitch from the front.

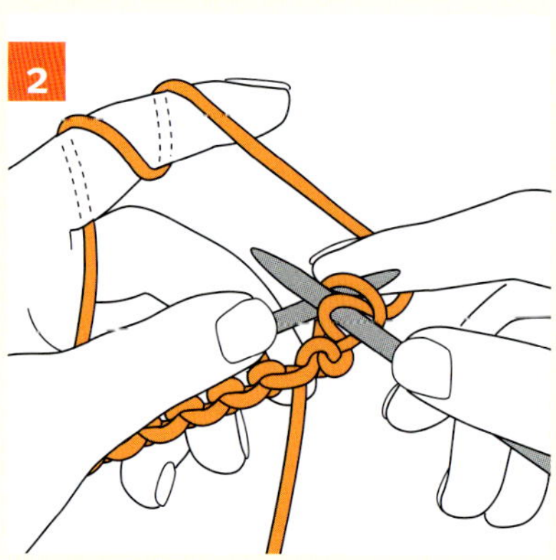

Then take the yarn with the right needle and pull through the stitch. Then slide the stitch of the preceding row from the left needle.

Knit 2 Stitches Together

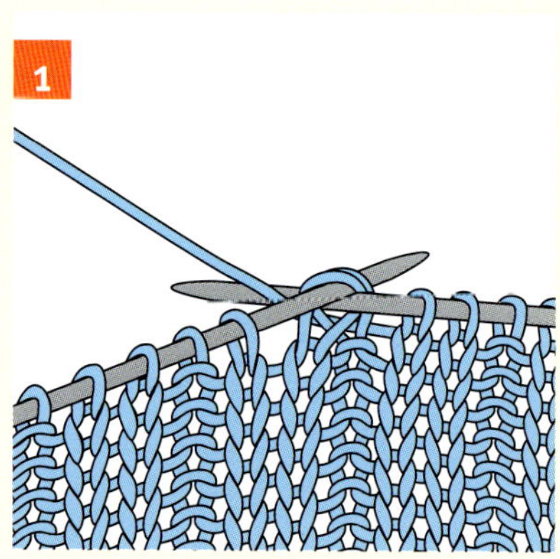

Place the yarn behind the work. With the right needle, take from left to right through both stitches, draw the yarn through. Slide the stitches from the left needle.

Purl Stitches

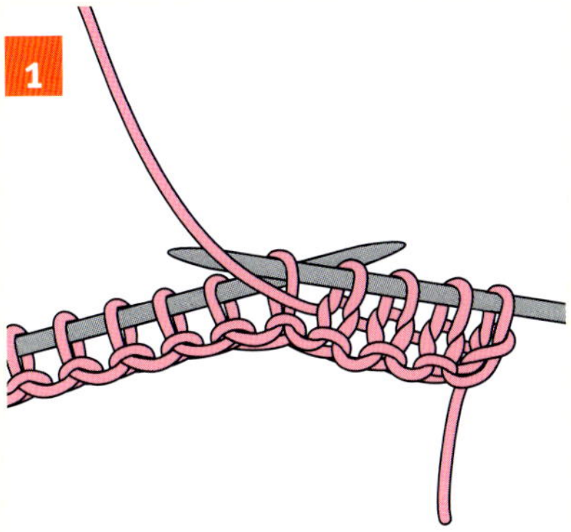

Place the yarn in front of the work, and with the right needle, insert into the stitch on the left needle from right to left.

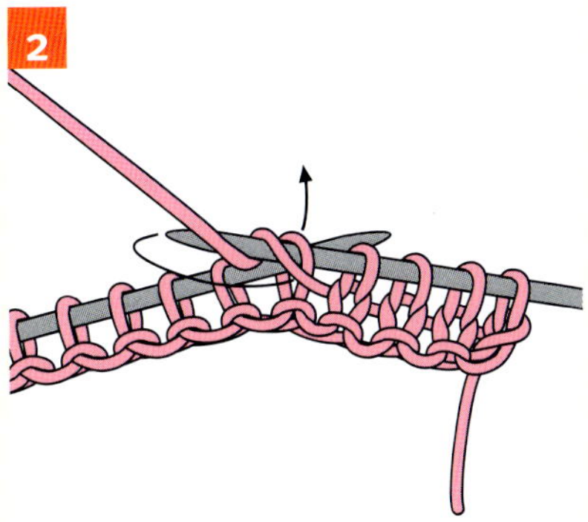

Wrap the yarn around the tip of the needle from the front to the back and draw through the stitch. Slide the stitch from the left needle.

Yarn Over

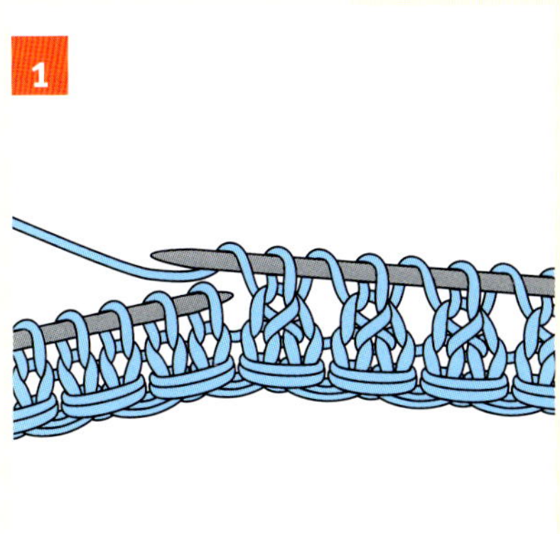

To work a yarn over means: Place the yarn over the right needle from the front to the back. Then continue working as specified in the respective instructions.

Casting Off Stitches

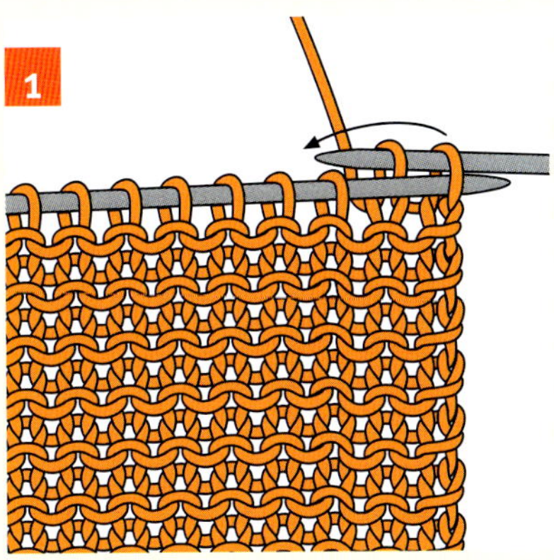

Knit the first 2 stitches. Take into the 1st stitch with the left needle, lift this over the 2nd stitch, at the same time pulling the 2nd stitch through the 1st with the right needle.

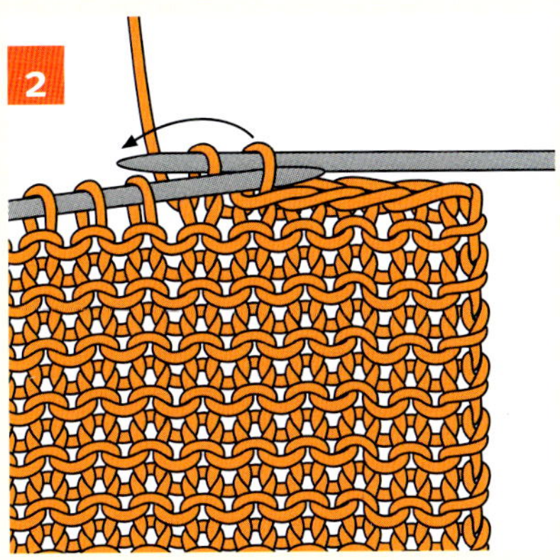

Knit the next stitch and pull over the previous one. Once all stitches are cast off, cut off the yarn and pull through the last stitch.

Pass Slip Stitch Over

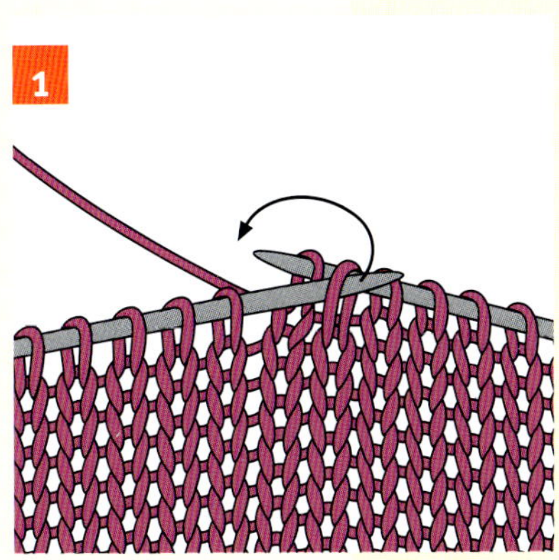

Slip, knit, pass slipped stitch over: Slip one stitch, knit the following stitch, and pass the slipped stitch over.

Basic Course in Crocheting

Cast On Chain Stitch

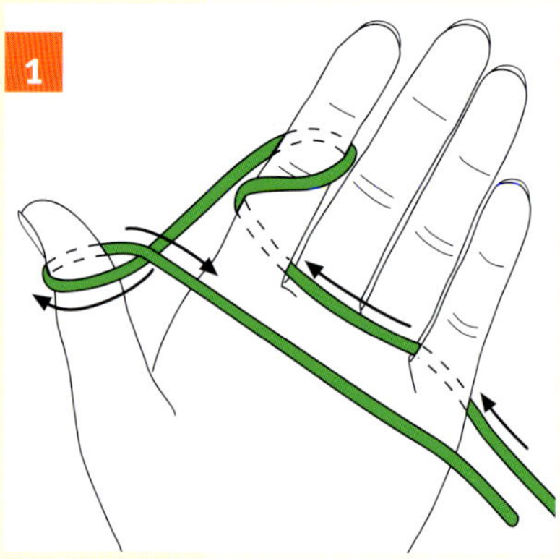

Place the yarn around the left hand as is shown in the picture.

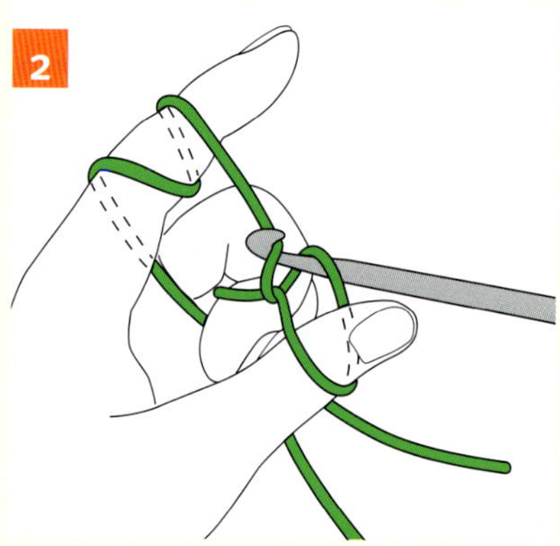

Insert the hook in the thumb loop from below. Catch the yarn and pull through. Take the thumb from the loop. The cast on knot and a loop are finished.

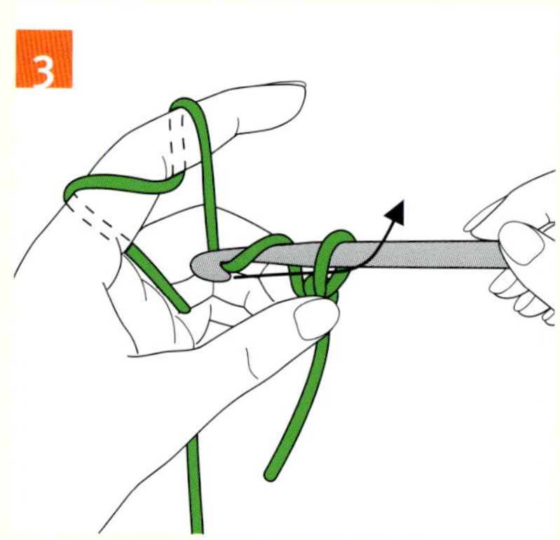

Hold the cast on knot with the thumb and middle finger, catch the yarn from the index finger with the hook, and pull through the loop; the 1st chain stitch is complete. For all others always repeat step 3.

Single Crochet Stitch

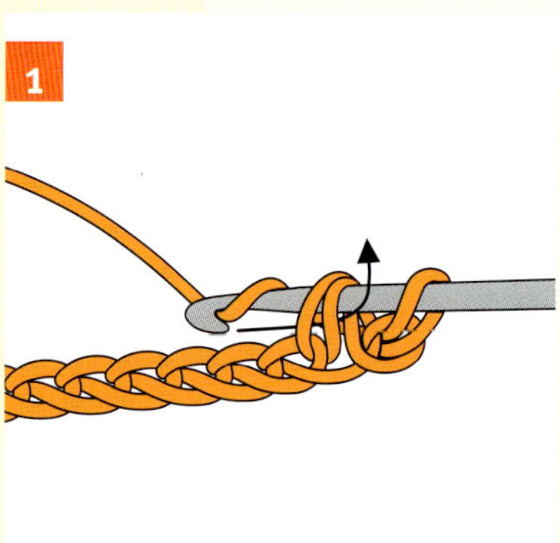

Insert into the 2nd chain stitch from the hook; place the yarn from the back to the front around the hook. Pull this yarn over through the chain stitch.

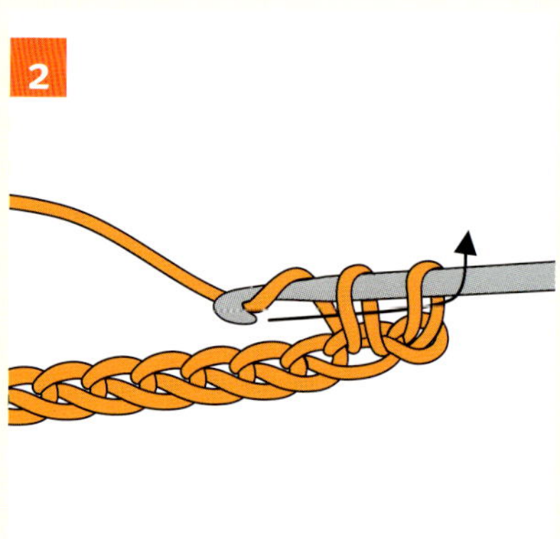

Newly, yarn over and pull through both loops on the hook. Repeat steps 1 and 2 for the following stitches.

Slip Stitch

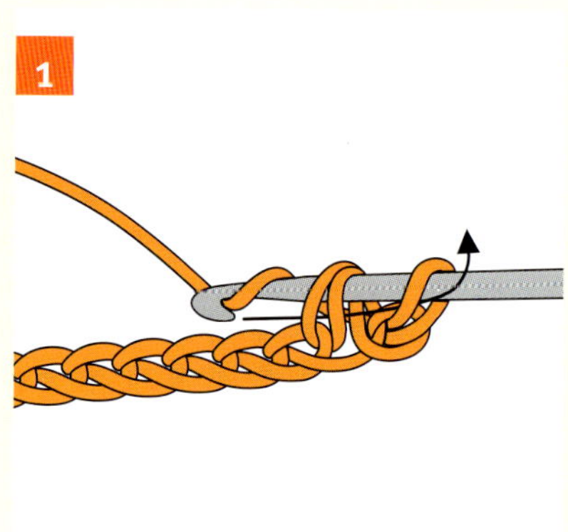

Insert into the 2nd stitch from the hook; place the yarn around the hook. Pull this yarn over through the stitch and loop that are on the hook.

Double Crochet Stitch

1

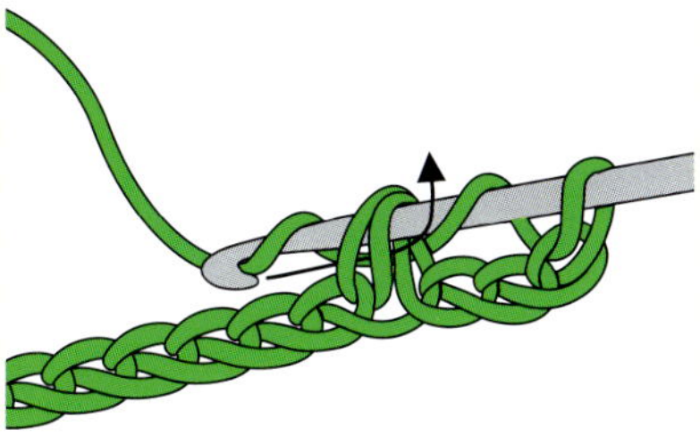

Yarn over the hook and insert into the planned stitch. Additionally, yarn over the hook and pull this through the stitch.

2

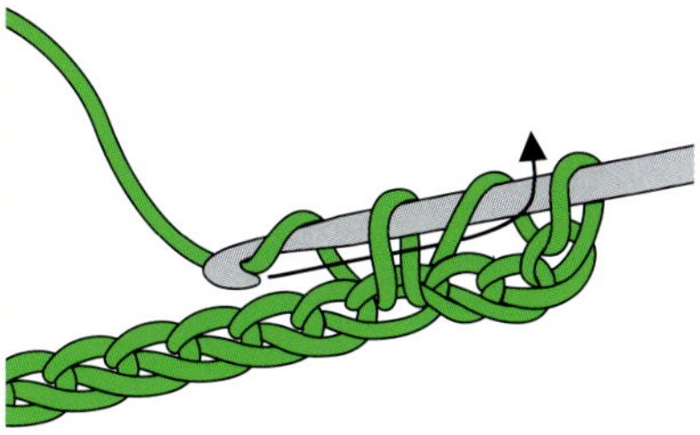

Newly, yarn over the hook and pull this through the first 2 of the 3 loops on the hook.

3

Yarn over the hook again and pull this through the remaining 2 loops on the hook.

Bobble

1

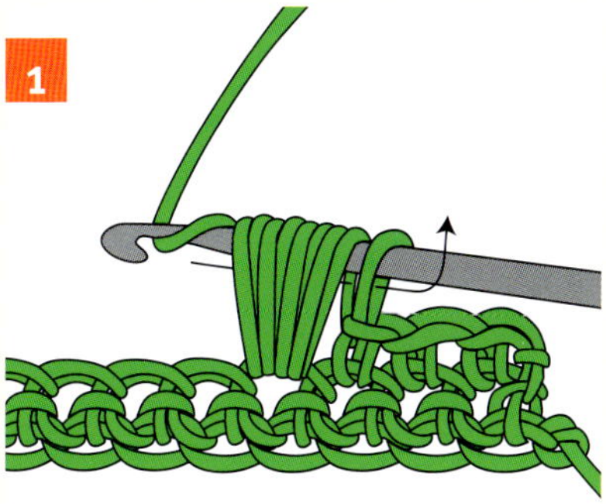

*1 yarn over, insert into the planned, always same stitch, 1 yarn over, pull through and up.
* Repeat 3 times. Newly yarn over.

2

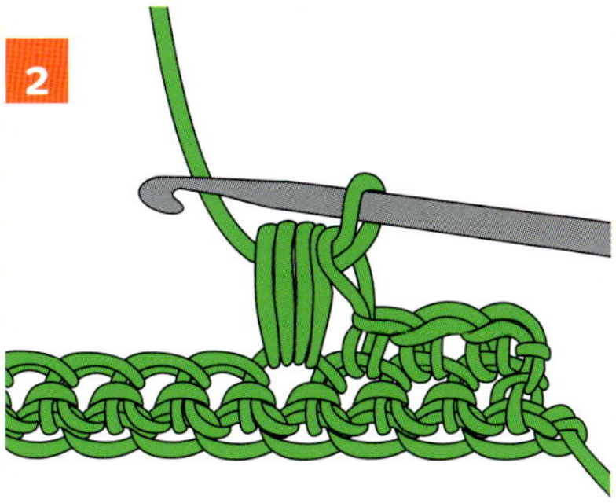

Pull the new yarn over through all of the loops on the hook. For this bobble it is 9 loops. Then close the bobble with 1 chain stitch.

Reverse Single Crochet

1

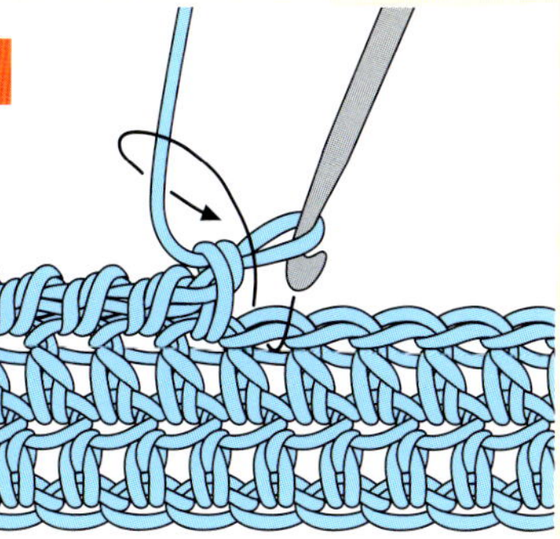

Reverse single crochets "run backwards," which means single crochet stitches are crocheted from left to right. Thus, an attractive corded edge is formed.

Notes

Notes

Notes